Also by Wendy Wasserstein

Bachelor Girls: A Collection of Essays

The Heidi Chronicles and Other Plays

The Sisters Rosensweig

Pamela's First Musical

An American Daughter

Shiksa Goddess

Shiksa Goddess

or, How I Spent My Forties

ESSAYS BY

Wendy Wasserstein

ALFRED A. KNOPF   NEW YORK 2001

Most of the pieces in this collection were originally published in slightly different form in the following publications:
Allure: *"Good, Better, Bette."*
Harper's Bazaar: *"Waif Goodbye, Hello Bulge," "Making Nice," "Poles Apart."*
New Woman: *"How to Do a Hollywood Awards Ceremony,"*
"My Low-Fat Dinner with Jamie Lee Curtis," "Women Beware Women,"
"The Muse That Mewed," "The Me I'd Like to Be."
New York Times: *"A Place They'd Never Seen: The Theater," "Hillary Clinton's Muddled Legacy," "Wendy's Workshop," "Ah, That First Feast in Wild Manhattan," "Dear Broadway, This Isn't Really Goodbye," "Directing 101: George Abbott on What Works," "Mom Says Every Day Is Mother's Day," "Theater Problems? Call Dr. Chekhov," "New York Theater: Isn't It Romantic."*
New York Times Magazine: *"She Saw Through Us."*
The New Yorker: *"Days of Awe: The Birth of Lucy Jane," "Shiksa Goddess," "The LUMP List," "First Ladies Get Dressed," "Don't Tell Mother," "Jill's Adventures in Real Estate," "Designing Men," "Heidi Chronicled."*
Slate: *"Diary."*
Stagebill: *"Three Sisters," "Afternoon of a Fan."*
Vogue: *"The Forty-eight-Hour Turnaround," "How Suite It Is."*
Washington Post: *"The Holiday Chronicles."*

For Ken Cassillo and Cindy Tolan

Contents

Preface

When I turned forty I made a To Do list composed mostly of items left over from when I turned thirty. The list included the annuals: lose weight, exercise, read more, improve female friendships, improve male friendships, become a better citizen. (The last was left over from my second grade To Do list.) At the end of my list were the larger-than-life unavoidables: move, fall in love, and the enormous "decide about baby."

Most of these essays were written in some pursuit of these quests. On assignment for *The New Yorker, Harper's Bazaar,* and the *New York Times,* I managed to focus my midlife obsessions. Looking over these essays, I seem to be the ideal candidate for a gender study on the interests of a forty-something, over-educated, (I hate to use the word) "nice" woman. My sense of irony, I hope, undermines the niceness.

I seem to continually write about politics, the arts, and women's equality. But I am not ashamed of my concurrent interest in real estate, diet, and my mother. In fact, my friends have told me how fortunate I am to have been born into so much material. I say it makes you many things; one is a bonanza for the mental health profession, and the other is a comic writer.

Most of these essays are comic, even satiric, in nature. But if the *New York Post* is going to run a headline "Oy Vey Hillary's Jewish," I can only respond that I'm really Episcopalian: a shiksa goddess. Of course as one travels further into midlife things become simultaneously more absurd and overwhelmingly real. I think of my sister Sandra thrilled with her weight loss due to chemotherapy. She died of breast cancer at age sixty.

At forty-eight I gave birth to my first child, a daughter, Lucy Jane. Due to complications she was born at twenty-six weeks' gestation. During the three weeks I spent in the hospital before her birth, and the ten weeks I spent visiting my baby in her intensive care neonatal unit, I realized that my day-to-day way of getting through it was partially due to the eye I developed as a comic essayist. I was able to survey the situation for every ridiculous anecdote while maintaining a nonsentimental center for what is truly important. Furthermore, it was my training in the theater that taught me to show up every day and hope for the best.

This collection ranges from a comic spoof on real estate agents to the birth of my daughter because I have come to know that comedy cannot be marginalized. It embraces the widest human conditions.

Acknowledgments

These essays were written over the course of ten years mostly for magazines and the *New York Times*. I would like to thank my dear friend and editor Betsy Carter, who gave me my first column in *New York Woman* and who brought me with her to *Harper's Bazaar* and *New Woman*. She is a consistent source of intelligent encouragement. David Kuhn took me to lunch at the Royalton and suggested that I write for *The New Yorker* when Tina Brown was editor of the magazine. He faxed me back after my first piece immediately. Writers dream about that.

At the *New York Times* I have been caringly edited by Mike Leahy, Sylviane Gold, and Andrea Stevens at the Arts & Leisure section. I am grateful to the Theatre Development Fund and the students at DeWitt Clinton High School, who gave me the privilege of taking them to the theater. Joanne Chen at *Vogue* sent the forty-eight-hour personal trainer to my house. I am still recovering. Mike Kinsley, at *Slate* magazine, keeps an eye out on not only the pieces I've written for him but all of my work. He has never had a problem with telling me "Why are you doing that?"

Susan Morrison and Dorothy Wickerdem at *The New Yorker* suggested that I write about the birth of my daughter. They were both remarkably articulate and sympathetic. David Remnick, the current editor of *The New Yorker*, has been encouraging and kind and knows the true meaning of a shiksa goddess.

Much more than an acknowledgment to Dr. Ian Holtzman and the neonatal intensive care unit at Mount Sinai Hospital. Without their first-rate care and the friendship of Gerald Gutierrez, William Ivey Long, Jane Rosenthal, Phyllis Wender, Flora Fraser, Peter Schweitzer, Rhoda Brooks, André Bishop, Peter Wolff, Tom Lynch, William Finn, Clifford and Betsy Ross, Daniel Swee, James Lapine, Heidi Ettinger, and my brother, Bruce Wasserstein, I would have never been able to write about my beautiful daughter, Lucy Jane.

Thanks to Judith Thurman for making me a home to write in and to the New York Society Library and the Cosmopolitan Club for their reassuring libraries to escape to. Nancy Novogrod at *Travel and Leisure* has sent me to spas and to Prague when libraries weren't a sufficient escape. Cathy Graham loves magazines more than anyone I know and in most cases she was the first to read these pieces. I am always indebted for her and her husband Stephen Graham's generosity and friendship.

My agents Lynn Nesbitt and Eric Simonoff have been beyond patient. Ten years is a long time to wait for a book. At Knopf, thanks to my editor Victoria Wilson, who witnessed my mother standing up when my name was called as a judge at the Broadway Cares/Equity Fights AIDS Easter bonnet competition. Nothing escapes Victoria Wilson and that's a gift to any writer. Dame Edna, the sage comedic superstar, once wryly described Stephen Sondheim as "the least complicated man I ever met!" The same can be said for Sonny Mehta. His friendship and wisdom is extraordinary.

This book would not exist without the assistance, kindness, and efficiency of Angela Trento and her friend Megan Cariola. Finally, looking back over my forties, Ken Cassillo and Cindy Tolan have redefined for me loyalty and sustaining friendship.

Shiksa Goddess

Shiksa Goddess

cannot tell a lie. I feel compelled to bite the bullet and publicly reveal that I've just discovered my own denominational truth. I am Episcopalian.

I should have guessed a long time ago, because my parents never mentioned it. In fact, they hid it. They sent me to primary school at the Yeshiva Flatbush. It never crossed my mind that I was deliberately being isolated. On our classroom walls were portraits of Chaim Weizmann and Golda Meir in place of Dwight and Mamie Eisenhower. Our horror stories were not of being buried by Communists, but of being suffocated by nomad ham sandwiches.

We lived in a Jewish neighborhood in Flatbush. Our shopping strip included kosher butchers and Hymie's Highway Appetizers. For Sunday brunch, my mother produced bagels, belly lox, and cream cheese with scallions. Nobody told me that lox lived a double life as smoked salmon, or that herring could ever be kippered.

Even the Christmas holidays were a setup. Every year on Christmas Eve, we were on a jet to Miami Beach. There wasn't even a chance for us to watch the WPIX Channel 11 Yule log burning as the Mormon Tabernacle Choir sang "Silent Night."

We celebrated the holidays front-row center at the Versailles Room, with Myron Cohen warming up our crowd for Sammy Davis, Jr. Even our African-Americans were Jewish!

Until now, I've had a happy life thinking of myself as a Jewish writer. I came to accept that when my work was described as being "too New York" it was really a euphemism for something else. I belonged to a temple, and on my opening nights, my mother invariably told friends that she'd be much happier if it was my wedding. In other words, I had a solid sense of self. I knew exactly who I was.

Then the bottom fell out. I was speaking at the Lion of Judah luncheon in Palm Beach recently when I noticed a woman in a Lilly Pulitzer dress, one strand of pearls, and forty-year-old pink Pappagallo shoes leaning against the door. She stood out from the crowd because, instead of the omnipresent Barry Kieselstein-Cord purse with lizard clasp, she was carrying a battered lacrosse stick.

At the conclusion of my talk, she approached the podium. "I hope you don't mind my speaking to you, but I believe we are related," she said.

I looked at her dead-straight blond hair and smiled politely. "I doubt it."

"Your name translates to Waterston," she continued. "Harry Waterston, your great-uncle twice removed, was my mother's fourth husband. They were married for one month." She looked at me as if only a simpleton wouldn't make the immediate connection.

I did have a distant relative, Dr. Harry Wasserstein, but I never heard of him marrying anyone but Aunt Rivkah. According to my mother, even though Harry was an educated man, he never worked a day in his life, and Rivkah's life was miserable.

"I think you must be mistaken," I said, and tried to excuse myself.

"After he left my mother, Harry Waterston changed his name to Wasserstein because he wanted his son to go to an Ivy League college, and to Mount Sinai Medical School. Harry Jr. became an educated man, but he never worked a day in his life."

I was *shvitzing.* I mean sweating. "Our name actually translates to Waterstone," I said.

"That's irrelevant!" She was almost haughty. "Look at that actor on *Law & Order*—what's his name, Sam? He's a Hasid if I ever saw one."

She handed me the lacrosse stick while I made a mental note to find out what Sam Waterston was doing for the High Holy Days. "This was Harry's lacrosse stick, which he used the year he was expelled from Hotchkiss," she said. "He made me promise to give it to the first Wasserstein relative I met in Palm Beach. He said it was inevitable that one of you people would show up here!" She winked and left the room.

Good or bad news had always made me hungry. But for the first time in my life I needed a drink. Maybe she was onto something.

That week, I began eating chicken sandwiches with mayo on white bread, no crust, and getting full after two bites. For the first time in my life, I wrote in to the *Mount Holyoke Quarterly:* "Am looking to buy thirty-year-old Saab car and to apologize to all the Holyoke girls named Timothy and Kikky, whom I never spoke to. I now know you were very interesting people."

I began wearing faded cardigan sweaters and canceled all appointments for massages, pedicures, and exploratory liposuction. I gave up on my complicated relationship with a married Jewish Malaysian vibes player and learned to enjoy the company of a divorced asexual friend from Amherst who studies pharmaceutical stocks for J. P. Morgan. I began running ten miles every morning and sculling down the Hudson nightly. My approval ratings with my friends have gone up fifteen points.

But I was still, as I used to say in Yiddish, *"nit ahin nit aher,"* or, as I now say in the Queen's English, "neither here nor there."

That was when I decided to go on a listening tour of Fishers Island. I wanted to really hear the stories of my new Wasp ancestors, learn to make their cocktails, and wear their headbands. I want to live up to my true destiny and announce to the world how great it is to be *goyisheh* like me.

A Place They'd Never Seen:
The Theater

As far as I'm concerned, every New Yorker is born with the inalienable right to ride the D train, shout "Hey, lady!" with indignation, and grow up going regularly to the theater. After all, if a city is fortunate enough to house an entire theater district, shouldn't access to the stage life within it be what makes coming of age in New York different from that in any other American city?

I am certain that I became a playwright because every Saturday my parents picked me up from the June Taylor School of Dance and brought me to a Broadway matinee. Of course, at the time I had no idea that I would even remotely have a life in the theater. No adult said to me, "Oh, Wendy, darling, don't become a doctor, a lawyer, or a certified public accountant. Please do us a favor and consider the not-for-profit theater." But watching those plays while I was still in high school first put into my mind the idea that the work you grew up to do didn't have to be entirely separate from your real interests.

As the 1998–99 theater season officially ended with the recent Tony Awards, and as the attendant hoopla is replaced by the weary question of where will the new audiences come

from, I have some good news from the front. Perhaps there is
even a glimmer of hope for the new season from eight New
York City high school students who have decided to make
theatergoing a habit.

Sadly, a New York adolescent's life as a regular theatergoer
is becoming the exception to the rule. Ticket prices have made
a family habit like mine almost an impossibility. Moreover,
those against government subsidy for the arts have marginalized theater as elitist and solely for the upper middle class.

Well-paid movie-marketing experts have endless figures and
charts to demonstrate that teenagers would far rather sit
through 10 *Things I Hate About You,* the movie remake of *The
Taming of the Shrew* set at a high school, than the Shakespeare
play itself.

While I was on a recent trip to Congress to lobby for the
arts, a senator asked if I was serious that theater was as important as health and education. I was tempted to say, "Yes, let
them eat plays!" But instead I hatched an idea to personally
bring New York high school students into the theater.

I mentioned my plan to Roy Harris, who was the stage
manager for my last three plays. Roy was quick to jump on
board: "Best thing you can do is get those kids in here. This is
audience development at the grassroots level!"

Stage managers are wonderfully organized people. One day
I'm daydreaming, and the next thing I know we're at a meeting at The Theatre Development Fund. Among its many func-
tions, the nonprofit TDF runs the half-price TKTS booth on
Broadway and works to develop new audiences.

"You get me eight smart high school students from the
New York City public school system and Roy and I will take
them to plays for a year," I proposed to Marianna Houston
Weber, the fund's director of education. "Just make sure it's no
one who is looking to get an agent or meet Drew Barrymore. I

want students who have never been to the New York theater, and let's see if it's at all still relevant to them."

Being a Brooklyn girl, I was hoping to include students from every borough. But Marianna said that the development fund already had a playwriting program set up with DeWitt Clinton High School in the Bronx. She offered to get in touch with Patricia Bruno a popular English teacher there, who would pick eight candidates from the accelerated math and science program.

DeWitt Clinton High School, named for the nineteenth-century New York mayor and governor, is the alma mater of the comedian Robert Klein, the designer Ralph Lauren, and the writers James Baldwin and Avery Corman. Over the years, the mix of the school's immigrant population has changed, but the commitment of teachers like Mrs. Bruno to opening worlds for their students has remained constant.

In September 1998, with the help of our educational advisers, Roy and I mapped out a more precise academic plan. We would see seven matinees: a potpourri of Broadway, off-Broadway, musicals, and straight drama. After each, we would go out for pizza and talk about the show. The students would be selected based on an essay about why the project interested them. Those chosen would keep a yearlong journal, for which they would receive high school credit.

On a cold Sunday in early November, the DeWitt Eight and Mrs. Bruno meet us for the first time in front of the Gershwin Theater to see George C. Wolfe's production of the musical *On the Town*. As our three boys and five girls ride the escalator upstairs, all in blue jeans with backpacks, I see Adolph Green walking across the lobby.

"That man wrote this show with his partner, Betty Comden, fifty-five years ago," I say, pointing him out to Manuel Nuñez and Omar Mendez. "He's the local talent, too."

We sit in the upper balcony, and as the orchestra begins to play "New York, New York," the eight students lean forward. I feel a lump forming in my throat. Immediately I think of Kenesha Johnson's application essay. She, like most of the others, mentioned wanting to have a sense of why it is good to live in New York before she left for college.

Yscaira Jimenez, an ebullient young woman, is immediately laughing and snapping her fingers to the Leonard Bernstein score. Watching the stage from her point of view, I am grateful for George Wolfe's commitment to diverse casting. All of my eight theatergoers are members of minority groups. At least this *On the Town* resembles their town, too.

Leaving the theater and bouncing down the street, Yscaira is singing "New York, New York." Later, she writes in her journal, "Seeing New York through the eyes of an outsider made me realize that I have so much of the world so close to me, which others just dream of having."

Over pizza, they tell me how modern the music seems. None of them has heard of Leonard Bernstein. I try to explain the plot and the phenomenon of the Miss Subways contest, and they giggle at the naiveté of it. What I don't learn until later is that most of the DeWitt Eight had anticipated that going to the theater would be a stiff and dreary affair. "Previous to my seeing this performance, I expected the theater to be boring and only for the rich and elegant," Manuel wrote in his journal after seeing *On the Town*.

Although they all say they enjoyed the show, when I ask if they would recommend *On the Town* to friends, they are silent. Omar emphatically shakes his reversed-baseball-capped head: "Oh, no! It's not cool to go to plays. I almost didn't try to sign up for this because I was afraid of what my friends would say. You know, stuff like 'the big classy thug.' "

Our next outing is to Beth Henley's lyrical play *Impossible*

Marriage starring Holly Hunter at the Roundabout. Beth Henley has found one of her greatest fans in the sensitive Kenesha.

"I loved the language in this play," Kenesha gushes about Ms. Henley's Southern-eccentric characters. "I could see beyond Holly Hunter's character's camouflage. You have to understand it's poetry!"

Chung Nguyen, on the other hand, found *Impossible Marriage* to be quite distressing. Chung, who came to America at age ten from Vietnam, feels the comic elements only diminish the seriousness of the moment. Of course, Chung himself is rather serious. He is the class valedictorian. What all the students do agree on, however, is that most of the audiences at our matinees are old and white. Erica Vargas, a shy and studious girl with wire-rim glasses, believes the DeWitt Clinton students stand out because of their age, their color, and their dress. Kenesha begins to worry that only whites go to the theater.

They are all relieved by the diversity of the audience at *The Trial of One Shortsighted Black Woman vs. Mammy Louise & Safreeta Mae,* directed by Paul Carter Harrison at the Henry Street Settlement's Abrons Arts Center. In fact, Kimberly Ebanks, the confident sophomore in our group, weeps throughout Marcia L. Leslie's play. She would later write in her journal, "I had no urge to wipe my tears away because it felt as though I was cleansing my soul and cleaning away the dirty film that slavery had left on me." Kimberly's catharsis was everything Aristotle dreamed it could be.

None of them had been to Lincoln Center prior to our Christmas visit to see *Parade,* the Alfred Uhry–Jason Robert Brown musical. As we walk through the Vivian Beaumont lobby, I tell them my play *The Sisters Rosensweig* had opened downstairs. I suddenly soar in their estimation.

Parade sweeps our crowd for outstanding theatrical event of the season. They are shocked to find out it was based on the real story of Leo Frank's lynching in Atlanta in 1915, and that such injustice could happen to a white Jewish man in the South.

As I take them backstage for our pizza and discussion, they poke one another when they recognize an actor. There are squeals of laughter as wigs and a peg leg pass by.

"How did they know to make such a serious subject into a musical?" Omar asks me.

"Have you ever heard of Hal Prince?" I respond. Their faces stare at me blankly. "He's the director, and for decades he has tried to stretch the boundaries of musicals. This time, he's working with a twenty-eight-year-old composer. So in many ways it's a merger of old-time theater craft with youthful innovation." I am hoping they get my analogy to our own cross-generation collaboration.

"I give it a nine and a half on a scale of ten," says Camille Darby, a sophomore and an aspiring playwright.

The others begin shaking their heads: "Ten!" "Ten!" "Eleven!"

"You know, no movie executive who decides what people your age are going to like would ever dream that *Parade* would mean so much to you," I say, smiling.

Yscaira is indignant. "They don't know about us! They think they do, but they don't."

We visit Lincoln Center again in February to see A. R. Gurney's play *Far East,* a memoir of a young naval officer's stint in Japan in 1954. The play is directed by Daniel Sullivan and Roy Harris is the stage manager. Roy takes us backstage and explains the intricacies of calling all the cues for the show and exactly what it takes to keep a play in shape night after night.

Erica writes in her journal, "The intensity of live theater is like a wild rush that one can almost never achieve from movies or literature."

Our most heated debate takes place after seeing Kenneth Lonergan's *This Is Our Youth*. It is about three young disaffected and privileged New Yorkers, one of whom is named Warren.

Omar is really ticked off: "Girls always fall for jerks like Warren."

The usually silent Erica jumps on him: "That's not true!"

Manuel defends his friend on the day of his eighteenth birthday: "Oh, you just feel sorry for him cause he's a spoiled rich kid who's wasting his life on drugs."

Kimberly jumps in: "I know plenty of people like Warren who aren't rich and are wasting their lives, too, you know."

For the first time, Marianna, Patricia, Roy, and I are silent. These are the experts. This is their youth.

Our final selection is a field trip to my own play *An American Daughter*, directed by Derek Anson Jones at the Long Wharf Theatre in New Haven. The students had earlier read the play and, for the most part, were not initially drawn to the story of a woman's embattled nomination for surgeon general.

Since their reading, however, I had revised the play significantly from the version that initially ran in 1997, emphasizing the political arguments and clarifying certain characters' motivations. Mr. Jones gave the play an edgy, almost Shavian interpretation. It was a production I was personally very pleased with.

When they return from the performance, which I had to miss, we meet at the V & T Pizzeria, a New York hangout even in my youth, adjacent to Columbia University.

First, there was college news. Yscaira was on her way with

a full scholarship to Columbia, Chung was waiting to hear about his financial aid from Haverford, and Erica from Barnard. Kenesha will be extolling *Impossible Marriage* at the University of Rochester, while Omar will hang his cap at SUNY–Albany.

Manuel was waiting to hear about his financial aid at SUNY–New Paltz.

"When I get to college, I'm going to see as many plays as I can," Chung tells me.

"Yes," I say, slyly, "but let's talk about what's really important here. What did you think of my play before you run off to all those others?"

They all agree that it was odd seeing the play because of their knowing me. "Did you think it was much angrier than I seem?" I ask. "No, it was funny," Chung answers. "I just couldn't find you in it."

Erica speaks up for my work: "I thought the play was very contemporary. The issues about women in this play made me think what it will be like for me." I want to kiss her.

She will write in her journal, "Women have always been oppressed by society, but sometimes it is the choice of women to let themselves be oppressed."

We begin taking photographs and toasting our theatrical season, which is coming to an end. "Do you think TDF should continue with this 'Wendy Project'?" Marianna asks the group.

Yscaira doesn't hesitate: "Absolutely!"

Omar gives two thumbs up—"Every inner-city student deserves this experience"—and vows that when he and Manuel settle in at college, they will go to plays often.

Yscaira wants to study theater history. Camille and Kimberly want not only to see plays but to develop their own artistic voices.

Someone pipes up: "My mother thinks we see the same play every week. She says, 'Go with your la-di-da friends.' But I wouldn't miss it. I just want to see more.'

Rather than speaking, Erica writes eloquently in her journal: "When I first began, I thought that theater was out of my league because only rich, white, old people went to see it. Broadway is no longer intimidating to me. I no longer feel like an outsider. This is especially important because I have lived in New York all of my life and this is the first that I am learning about what is standing in my own backyard."

Frankly, going to plays with them made me also feel less of an outsider from my city and my own work. I, too, learned who is standing in my own backyard.

Kimberly Ebanks summed up our program in a speech before New York City high school teachers: "Seeing plays has changed me from a student who believed that in order to be successful in life I had to excel only in math and science. Life isn't only about math and science. It's about hypocrisy, prejudice, love, joy, compromise, hate, and conflict. These are things that are not only found in life but in theater itself."

My favorite high school history teacher told us that the way to start a revolution was to seize the means of production. Perhaps one way to revolutionize the theater is for its artists to become responsible for not only what is on the stage but who in the future will be sitting in the theater.

This project will continue next year, as a joint venture of the Theatre Development Fund and the League of American Theatres and Producers. Financing has been made available for three New York City high school groups, including DeWitt Clinton.

To anyone who doubts the relevance of contemporary theater, I would say just ask the DeWitt Clinton Eight. Certainly Manuel's fear that theater would prove to be boring was happily unfounded. The art form was gloriously compelling. Now the trick is to eliminate "only for the rich and elegant." If the price was right—which is not only a high school student's dream—and the theater truly became the undisputed birthright of every New Yorker, it would be way cool, indeed.

Hillary Clinton's Muddled Legacy

illary Rodham, in her 1969 Wellesley College commencement address, eloquently summed up the hopes of her generation: "We're searching for more immediate, ecstatic, and penetrating modes of living. . . . Every protest, every dissent, is unabashedly an attempt to forge an identity in this particular age."

That idealistic, forthright Hillary is gone—one of the saddest and most destructive consequences of the Monica Lewinsky scandal. In her place is a new Hillary, loyal wife. And according to a recent New York Times/CBS News poll, 73 percent of Americans now approve of her. Her approval rating is at a record high, even as her actual achievements are at a record low.

As a 1971 graduate of Mount Holyoke College, I have always been struck by the fact that the three most recent first ladies had all attended women's colleges. Both Barbara Bush and Nancy Reagan did a stint at Smith, and Hillary Rodham graduated from her alma mater with flying colors. Like their Seven Sisters classmates, all three women were trained to develop an independent intellect as well as the grace to serve living room teas.

Though I am not a close friend of Mrs. Clinton, I have had the pleasure of making her acquaintance on several occasions, including a dinner at my brother's house two weeks ago. In 1993, at an intimate supper for one hundred (the guests included Toni Morrison and Julia Roberts), I watched in awe as the newly installed first lady confidently whispered to the head waiter when to begin serving the dessert.

I had no idea where this graduate of Yale Law School and children's rights advocate could possibly have picked up such a skill. But then I remembered dressing for "Gracious Living," a semiweekly ritual at Mount Holyoke that consisted of formal dinners, complete with waitresses and folded cloth napkins. I'm sure Wellesley had its equivalent when Hillary Rodham was a student, too.

But the times were changing. When I entered college in 1967, the first lady's junior year, it was not uncommon for students to describe themselves as "hoping to marry Harvard." By 1970, women's history was being taught at Mount Holyoke with a syllabus that included books by Betty Friedan and Germaine Greer.

Women like Hillary Rodham suddenly had the same career opportunities as the men they were supposed to wed. Marriage would be for love or companionship, but would no longer be a substitute for individual destiny.

If anyone's life would have been transformed by the burgeoning women's movement, it should have been hers. Ask any Yale Law School graduate of that era and he or she will remember the brilliance and ambition of Hillary Rodham. She was an activist, a student leader, someone with a great sense of civic responsibility. She was the hope for a new definition of professional women.

Not that anyone thought it would be easy. My college classmate Harriet Sachs, who started a women's law firm in

Toronto, told me recently, "Hillary is a traditional figure." In fact, Mrs. Clinton has used those very words herself to describe her role in America's political landscape. Sadly, however, her current popularity seems a bridge to the past rather than the future.

The wife of the presidential candidate who told a CBS interviewer in 1992 that "I'm not some little woman standing by my man like Tammy Wynette" is now being applauded for doing precisely that. The first lady who dared to take on health care reform has now been diminished to a popular soap opera heroine. Maintaining the dignity of her marriage, difficult as that may be, is now seen as her greatest professional triumph.

Of course, she may have no choice—what else would anyone have done in such a situation? But the truth is, long before anyone had ever heard of Monica Lewinsky, Hillary Rodham Clinton was hardly a feminist icon. She has always sent confusing signals.

She has flip-flopped on so many issues of image that her behavior can justifiably be called erratic. First she defiantly wasn't baking cookies, then suddenly we were barraged with her recipes for Christmas cookies. Initially she sandwiched "Rodham" within her name, and then it magically disappeared. When the coast was clear, it slinked back out again. Her husband implied she'd be copresident, a first-rate two-for-one bargain. Then her health care reform package failed, and she retreated.

Now, the impressive personal qualities—idealism, strength, and poise under pressure—that she once directed toward influencing social policy are being used to maintain domestic tranquillity.

Sadly, the messages being sent to the younger generation of women are that "you can't have it all" and "don't expect too much." The name Hillary Rodham Clinton no longer stands for self-determination, but for the loyal, betrayed wife. She is moving further and further away from her role model, Eleanor Roosevelt, who used her perch as first lady to be an independent advocate.

Indeed, Mrs. Clinton's high approval ratings means she's currently appealing to a constituency—older, more conservative women—that had never supported her. Those who were threatened by a first lady who was aggressive and professional are impressed by her ability to keep the home fires burning in dire circumstances. Pity and admiration have become synonymous.

One hopes this will not be the end result. It's certainly not what all the feminists who have stood by Bill Clinton intended. One instinctively knows this is not what Hillary Clinton intended.

Personally, I wish the talented Hillary Rodham Clinton would stand up and sign in please. We women of her generation had hoped she would break new ground. Yet what seemed initially so positive is becoming a very unsavory parable.

The Forty-eight-Hour Turnaround

was born to order up. During my entire Manhattan child-hood, my mother never made a cup of coffee. We ordered up breakfast exclusively from the local Lexington Avenue Greek coffee shops. My favorite breakfast china has always been a paper cup embossed with a picture of the Parthenon.

In adult life, I have followed my mother's recipes for good old-fashioned home cooking. My refrigerator remains an empty cavern with the occasional six-pack of diet Coke and ancient lettuce from a long-past attempt at a healthier life. My personal chefs are reachable only by telephone at the neighbor-hood Chinese and Italian restaurants. I am a walking magnet for fats, sugars, and useless carbos.

My childhood fitness routine was of the Broadway variety. Every Tuesday and Saturday I took ballet, jazz, tap, and acro-batics classes. To this day, I can not only recognize a proper hitch kick but also instruct any novice how to do one well.

At around age twelve, however, when it became clear that my legs weren't going to begin somewhere around my shoul-ders, I suddenly preferred doing homework to time steps. I became the perfect dance potato: a playwright. My idea of a great opening number is sitting at my desk and imagining one. My favorite exercise took all the abdominal strength of getting from sitting to sleeping position.

Every now and then, however, I do attempt to turn over a new leaf. I take myself out of my home to some health spa in a tropical or southwestern locale, and vow to forgo all of my favorite things. These disciplined regimens of steamed red peppers and early-morning walks have a very short shelf life. At least twenty-four hours after leaving the canyons, the beach, or the mountain of health and tranquillity, I am inevitably stressed out, prone, and dialing for cheeseburgers. After forty-eight hours, I am, in fact, so anxious that I am speed dialing.

Recently I came to the conclusion that perhaps if I brought Mohammed to the mountain I could make a more significant lifestyle change. In other words, instead of compartmentalizing my time into two weeks of healthy living on a ranch, I would incorporate those two weeks into my daily urban routine. This is how I persuaded myself to open my door to Sue Rue, the twenty-four-hour "I have a little shadow that goes in and out with me" personal live-in trainer.

Admittedly, it takes a certain kind of desperation to sign on for twenty-four-hour nutritional and exercise surveillance. And there are other alternatives. A woman in Omaha was rumored to have wired her lips together and lived on wheatgrass juice. An actress in West Hollywood chained herself for seventy-two hours to a Versa-Climber. But for those of us whose nutritional resolutions begin at breakfast and fade by midmorning coffee, Sue Rue is on hand twenty-four hours to say, Stop! In the name of self-love. Like a proficient Mrs. Clean, she gets into where the excess dirt, grime, and grease are hidden. A twenty-four-hour trainer won't allow her clients to cross-train at the gym and then reward themselves at Pizza Hut. She will teach her clients that fitness is a full-time job.

Three days before Ms. Rue arrived, her shopping list appeared on my fax machine. As a single woman who has never turned on her Viking range, I was frankly bewildered as to what I would do with eight small crookneck yellow squash, twelve zucchini, and three bags of spinach. Parsley, mint, and shallots were pouring out of the vegetable bins. Even my cats were completely disoriented by the paper bags from the Food Emporium. Where, amid all this roughage, would I find something to eat?

Sue's home base is Michael's Body Scenes in Boca Raton, Florida, but like Wonder Woman she is extremely portable. She flies up to New York for our weekend boot-camp orientation.

A tall, leggy blonde, she arrives in my apartment at 4:00 p.m. on Friday wearing a black jogging suit and bearing an array of health-food-gourmet ginger marmalades. Ironically, she reminds me immediately of Mrs. Fields, the chocolate-chip entrepreneur: chignon, high cheekbones, perfect French manicure, and full of confident enthusiasm. It could be worse, I keep telling myself. I could have arranged to spend Valentine's Day weekend with Miss Universe or a midnight-aerobics teacher from a Hawaiian television station.

We carefully plot our weekend. She will be in my pocket like a biblical prayer, "when I lie down, and when I rise up." Sue Rue offers "tuck in" service before she returns nightly to her nearby hotel room. In many ways, Sue Rue, a certified personal trainer, is "Mother Health." She will be there to hold my hand and guide me. For those of us who were rebellious children, this kind of constant maternal attention might be even more disorienting than a fat-free weekend. Sue Rue has been known to rewrite entire family recipes so that they are low fat. She restocks kitchen cupboards and divides them up into adults' and kids' zones. College women hire her for long weekends to get them out of the freshman-fifteen rut. She will maternally advise how to make all of these life changes fit into your personal, professional, and even spiritual life. She is a fat-free beacon of light.

Sue evaluates my health history. She wants to know how I sleep, how I eat, and how I have incorporated time for myself into my life. I know as women we're all supposed to be eager to share immediately, but I am a little reluctant to talk about my personal life or family to a complete stranger. Of course, by now I am convinced she is thinking, Not only is this client sedentary and slightly yellow, she is also a psychosocially re-pressed nightmare. But Sue reassures me, "My goal is not to beat you up, but to very gently nudge you into the direction of good health." After her evaluation, she says that she sees me as a "walker/yoga/light-weights kinda lady." Why she didn't see me as a rock climber I just don't understand.

While Sue continues to size up my health habits, I get up my courage to ask her age. For a woman of roughly my own era, she looks unbelievably good. OK, I tell myself when she says she is fifty, Sue, just tell me what to do.

Saturday morning Sue arrives at my apartment promptly at seven-thirty and rings the doorbell. "Why me, O Lord, why me!" I pull my covers up. The doorbell rings again. She is obviously not going away. I answer in my pajamas. Sue asks me if I've eaten yet, and I want to tell her it's a triumph that I am even standing.

Before we go out, Sue prepares for me a small bowl of shred-ded wheat and fresh berries. She reminds me one more time about the empty calories of bagels and regular muffins. Per-haps I will spend my life in search of the nutritionist/trainer who believes, as I do, that giant carrot muffins are really a vegetable.

My friend William Finn, the Broadway composer/lyricist, joins us for our morning constitutional in Central Park. He immediately falls in love with Sue Rue. "This is fabulous!" he tells me. "I could have her take care of me twenty-four hours a day." There are people who crave attention and others who don't. I am definitely in the "I want to be alone" category. Therefore, unlike my dear friend Billy, I am not an ideal candidate for hands-on "Rue"dimentary conditioning.

After the walk we make our way to the World Gym on Broadway for a round of easy weight lifting. A small actual admission, a minor character flaw: I don't really mind exercising. Frankly, I frequent a cozy small gym on the East Side called Casa and run around the park with a trainer, Tom Imbo, the nicest man in the world.

Sue is definitely not overwhelmed by my weight-lifting abilities. I can sort of sustain two five-pound dumbbells. But my triceps have gone away for a permanent junior year abroad. Sue is by no means critical. This boot camp is not the hardcore division. Sue believes her job is to find the "little buttons" that make her clients tick. In my case, the button is clearly marked BE GENTLE.

In my desire to include a healthier regimen in my daily life, Sue has arrived on a day when I have to put the finishing touches on a long-due teleplay. As I am hysterically completing my work, she serves me the perfect spa lunch on a tray: vegetable soup and a salad of fresh tuna, mahimahi, sole, ginger, carrots, red and yellow peppers, and tomato on a bed of baby greens. Sue is a great cook. I could maybe learn to not want to be alone quite so much.

That afternoon I have a previous engagement to take my mother and my nephews to the matinee of *The Diary of Anne Frank*. My mother was the first woman on her block to send away for a Jack La Lanne Glamour Stretcher, a prehistoric version of the now popular elastic Dyna-Band. I also get Sue a ticket. This should be love at first sight.

"So you're going to teach Wendy how to eat," I overhear my mother say to Sue during intermission.

"We're going to get into that kitchen and start cooking," says Sue, smiling.

"You think you can fix her in a weekend?" my mother asks her.

Some girls just know how to have fun on Valentine's Day. I watch my nephew Ben purchase a packet of M&M's. I would give anything in the world for him to slip me one or two blues. Frankly, I'd give him two tickets to the musical of his choice for a brown one. But Sue is watching, and I know I mustn't mess with Mother Health. To the contrary, I suggest we walk the twenty blocks home. Do I want to impress Sue? Of course I do.

My assistant Ken Cassillo and I make plans for an emergency run to Federal Express while Sue prepares dinner. We're having butternut-squash soup, grilled swordfish, and two small red potatoes. I ask Sue if it's all right if we have a glass of wine. "On the weekends I allow my clients to play," she says, smiling at me.

We sit down to supper and Sue explains to me how she varies her approach for all her clients. From her point of view, I am someone who needs more downtime to reconnect to her body. Perhaps she is saying this because I am now lying exhausted on the kitchen floor. Sue offers to put me into bed and help me meditate, which by this point sounds divine. I had promised, however, to go dancing in the Bronx with a friend. When I call her to cancel, I feel unbelievably guilty. Therefore we make a secret compromise and whisper so my boot-camp counselor can't hear me.

Note: I am now admitting in print that I ran away from Camp Rue. Furtively, my friend Barbara Howard and I met at Petrossian restaurant for caviar and vodka at midnight. I feel Sue Rue's tears welling as she reads this. Sue, I should have been meditating!

Sunday morning Sue arrives at 8:00 a.m. to take me back to the gym. I am a little foggy, but she doesn't know why. She is amazed when I suggest all of my own accord that we sign up for my first-ever Spinning class. I feel I have to make things up to her.

Spinning is a way of life! The classroom of thirty bicycles is a semicircle filled with top-of-the-line bikers ready to pedal like hell on their one-way trip to nowhere. It seems to me the ultimate existential millennium journey. Wini, our body-building instructor from Queens, tells us, "It's your ride. You are responsible for it." These riders-in-the-dark hardly ever hit their stationary seats: they're up, they're down, they're sweating like crazy. I am riveted. Sue Rue is beside me. She keeps telling me to take another sip of water. She doesn't know that I am way beyond water. I am thinking I have landed on another planet. I know in my lifetime I will never be adjusting the resistance damper on that bicycle to make it harder to pedal. My own resistance is hard enough as it is. My calves are beyond quivering. But I stay my course.

Sue is very impressed I didn't drop out. But I know boot camp has gotten the best of me. Sue shows me how to make egg white, spinach, and tomato omelets with non-butter spray. I am so exhausted I ask her if we need to sauté the eggs in fruit juice first. I am desperate to go to bed and rest. We plan to take a late-afternoon yoga class. Sue believes that my flexibility and dance training would make me the perfect candidate for one-legged posing. I know she's right about paying attention to my needs and my breathing. But like Scarlett

O'Hara, I vow that "tomorrow is another day." I forgo yoga and get into bed.

Since I can't provide Sue with the challenge of a first-class fitness partner, I decide I can at least introduce her to some interesting New Yorkers. I invite Forrest Sawyer, the ABC anchorman, and Bill Finn and his friend Arthur Salvadore for dinner à la Rue. Sue grills vegetables on the Viking range, and we sit down to a giant bowl of salad and her Santa Fe pasta.

"I could eat like this every night!" Billy exclaims.

"You're sweet!" Sue smiles at him.

"No, it's true. Come live with me!" Billy is close to begging.

"I bet you hear that all the time," says Forrest, putting on his lower interview voice.

"I enjoy my work. But I need my downtime too." Sue politely ends the conversation. Personally, I wonder if Billy would be begging if he knew a weekend of Rue conditioning costs approximately fifteen hundred dollars. So whether you send yourself away to seek a nutritional Mohammed in a desert retreat or Mohammed comes to your own apartment, it costs roughly the same.

After our guests leave, Sue magically cleans up while I continue to rest from my day's activities. Sue Rue told me earlier that her clients are in many ways her children. I am now part of her extended family, the sedentary branch.

We don't have a long or teary farewell. But Sue is gracious and professional. She wishes she could get a hold of me on a more permanent basis. Oddly enough, I wish she could too. There is something to be said for someone who can be so concerned about whether I did or didn't avoid cheese that week.

Suddenly the potential for Sue's taking me everywhere I hate to go—mammograms, the accountant, jury duty—seems like a fairy tale come true. This is a personal trainer who will

attend to all the hideous details. Life could be a lot less tedious
with Sue around. I am immediately reminded of the Stephen
Sondheim lyric "No one is alone." I'd buy her a diamond just
for making me show up for a gum cleaning.

"You're a very special lady." She squeezes me. "Be good to
yourself."

I always get weepy when someone says "Be good to yourself." I want to turn and say in a very Noël Coward accent,
"But Sue, what will I do without you?"

A week after Sue returned to Boca Raton I received her formal evaluation. "Health: fair to good but needs to take better
care of herself." "Food: does not preplan her food and orders
in." "Exercise: needs an organized schedule to walk first thing
in the morning." In other words, I'd say I was a boot-camp
B minus/C plus. I tell myself that maybe if I had gone to that
yoga class I would have pushed my average up to a solid B.
Maybe if I hadn't coveted Ben's M&M's, Sue would have
described my health as better. If only she knew that last week,
at just about the 5:00 p.m. double latte and cookie time, I
thought of Sue and baked a potato with a delightful fat-free
Creole dip instead.

Since Sue's appearance, I have actually started to make a reasonable all-out effort. I do try to walk every day, eliminate
obvious fats, and at least remember that good health isn't only
the province of the swimsuit competition. Even Miss Congeniality deserves to feel good every now and then. There are still
Rue zucchinis and mushrooms filling up my refrigerator, and I
did make it to one yoga class.

Sue Rue would make a fine angel in a nineties nutritional
remake of *It's a Wonderful Life*. She could take us all on a tour of
what would happen if we didn't learn to cherish our pretty-
good health.

How Suite It Is

made a huge mistake. I bought an apartment. It's a great
New York apartment: sunlight, views, cozy kitchen, very
grown-up, very glamorous. It's everything a real estate bro-
ker could want for a girl. Except when you're a girl who really
wants to live in a hotel.

For one blissful year between apartments, I was Lulu at the
Lowell. The Lowell Hotel is conveniently located on Manhattan's fashionable Upper East Side, just three blocks from Barneys, one block from the Colony Club, and about fifteen
blocks from where I grew up. It's definitely a Freudian something to move into a hotel in your own backyard.

My room number was 6B. When the phone rang, a sophisticated voice answered, "The Lowell Hotel; how can I help
you?" As soon as my callers asked for me, Debbie the operator
would reply in the most accommodating upper-crust manner,
"With pleasure." No one has ever gotten that kind of reception when it was only me at the other end.

I'm simultaneously much too old and much too young to
live in a hotel. Eloise lived at the Plaza because she was six and
had no other choice. Ancient countesses retire to the Palace
Hotel in Lausanne to wear tiaras while watching Italian TV

game shows with other haunted aristocrats. But I am neither fallen aristocracy nor someone left behind to live with my nanny. I was just a writer with a few personal decisions to avoid and professional deadlines to make.

Hotel life in times of transition is completely manageable. I loved the chintz couches in my room that I had absolutely nothing to do with selecting. Even better, I have no idea who in the world grazed those cushions just before me. There were books on my shelf, assorted *Reader's Digest* anthologies and mysteries that I knew I would never crack. It's very soothing being surrounded by a life that's comfortable but doesn't resonate. My friends would inquire if I didn't yearn for my own things. I would explain that "my own things" and I were taking a much needed breather from each other. We were working on our relationship. My only possessions for that entire year were my clothes—enough for a week of day-into-evening looks—a few newly purchased books and CDs, and a typewriter. It was the luxury version of a dorm-room suite: a sort of junior year across the park. Life boiled back down to basics: work, friendship, and room service.

There are certain personal parameters for moving into the right hotel. Personally, I would have a very hard time setting up house at a Marriott or an airport Hyatt. The point of hotel life is discreet intimacy, not anonymity. Sheet-glass windows that resist opening seem a sure precursor to leaving one's mortal container behind. If only I were forty pounds lighter and twenty years younger, I would have considered a hipper joint like Miami's Delano or L.A.'s Mondrian. But who wants to think about age and weight right before dinner?

The Lowell is comfy, cozy, pricey, just like the better small English hotels. Tom and Phillip behind the desk always said hello. We'd chat briefly as if I were part of the family, but they never pried and neither did I. One snowy night, Jeff the porter

came up to light the fireplace in my room. Joe the Sunday telephone operator gave me a play he wrote, and Felicia the evening maid blessed me so many times that by now I suspect
my bed will be beautifully made in heaven. The owners, who
became my friends, would take me to dinner at the Post House,
the hotel's adjoining restaurant. He had an idea for a musical,
and she is my idol, a film producer whose children believe that
breakfast arrives from a menu. It's really the best sort of replica
family—warm, polite, without the guilt or pain. No real questions asked except the inevitable "When are you checking
out?"

Here are things you never have to do when you're living in a
hotel:

1. Order in from a takeout menu. Especially when
   room service has lemon-peppered chicken.
2. Find a dry cleaner or fresh towels.
3. Get to know your neighbors.
4. Go searching for scotch and vodka miniatures or
   five-dollar bags of potato chips.
5. Make decisions with a decorator and an architect.
6. Book a hotel room for an affair.
7. Believe your life is stuck. It's obviously in transition
   or you wouldn't be in a hotel.
8. Dwell on the past. Every day your bed is freshly
   made.
9. Dwell on the future. There isn't enough room in the
   suite for the future.
10. Avoid writing. A hotel room is as close as modern
    life comes to a monastery.

To be fair and not to seem completely spoiled and insane, I
did move into the hotel when I was desperate. My sublet had

ended prematurely, and I needed a place to live before construction was completed on the apartment I had bought. But of course the "suddenly separated" investment bankers who moved in at about the same time I did were in their own way desperate, too.

Those bachelors are now all remarried—it's a very short shelf life—and happily ensconced in their sea-foam Fifth Avenue duplexes. Whereas I still yearn for those carefree days with a stranger's shoes waiting to be polished in front of the room next door. However, I am training myself not to regret moving out. Instead I congratulate myself on becoming truly adult, having a monthly mortgage to pay, getting to really recognize the value of a Sub-Zero refrigerator and a Viking range, not to mention the subtleties of a perfectly constructed powder room. Now I believe I am entitled to place a call to my friends at the Lowell and ask "with pleasure" if they could get the terry robe with the insignia ready and tell Jeff to get the fire burning. Lulu's coming back to 6B for the weekend. After all, a girl needs a place to get down to serious work in order to pay for that Viking range.

The LUMP List

Dear Subscriber: For those of you who believe that the New Year really begins with the fall season, this list comes in the nick of time. Anyone who says there are no available men left just hasn't been doing her homework. Talk about diversity! This month's selection of Last Unattached Male Persons (LUMP) ranges from a triple-hot Hollywood agent to our favorite Kinko's copies operator, who's still holding on after ninety-six months on the List. We guarantee, as always, that our listees are completely unattached and willing to sit through at least the first course of dinner or Act One of a play. So move quickly! And take your lumps. The heart doesn't have to be a lonely hunter.

HOLLYWOOD HEAVEN First time on the list. Jonathan (Skip) Fine, 32, talent agent. Works from 6:00 a.m. until midnight and seldom returns calls. Enjoys cigars, three-hour weight-lifting sessions at the gym, and hanging out with clients. "I'm looking for a real relationship now," Jonathan has confided to the List. "Good relationships are the backbone of my business."

TWO-FOR-ONE ROYALTY SPECIAL This month only. Prince Andre and Prince Claude, 40, twin pretenders to the Transylvanian throne. The princes attended Rollins College, in Winter Park, Florida, for one semester and currently live in Gstaad, where they enjoy skiing, hiking, and duty-free shopping. "We pledge that one day our wife will be queen of an independent Transylvania—if her father pays for the castle." Both princes' eyes fill with tears. "Pick either of us, or both. We share *everything*."

A BOY A MOTHER COULD LOVE Bernard Lincoln Schwab, 46, divorced bond trader, is anxious to remarry, because all the major players have. "It's not enough to bring trophy women to benefits anymore," Link says he's learned. "I want to bring a trophy wife."

A DOCTOR IN THE HOUSE Dr. Luis Silver, Brazilian plastic surgeon, 36. This doctor can laser four inches from the hips and add it to a patient's height. Married three times, Dr. Silva is looking for a real woman with a warm heart. "Any woman can be made beautiful on the surface," Dr. Luis told us from his Beverly Hills clinic, "but genuine beauty comes from deep in the soul." Women over 120 pounds need not respond. Height over 5'7" preferably. Blue eyes. No contacts, please.

START FROM SCRATCH Ved Varajan, 34, Palo Alto multimillionaire, inventor of "Marscape," the first Internet link to Mars. Ved still lives in his Stanford dorm room and enjoys cybersex and computer solitaire. "I'm insecure, so I like to propose on the first date," says the never-married Varajan, whose net worth currently tops four hundred million. A genuine find.

MATURE AUDIENCES ONLY Former acid-rock drummer Theodore T. Jones, 48, recently cured his well-documented fear of intimacy and commitment with a mixture of Paxil, Midol, and Saint-John's-wort. Ted enjoys yoga and Rocky and Bullwinkle cartoons, and is looking for a calm, nonverbal, maternal woman over sixty-five. He admits, "I've been through a lot, and I'm not interested in going through any more."

OUR OWN ROOT-CANAL MAN Dr. Henry Weissblatt, 56, West Village dentist. Dr. Weissblatt never thought he was anything out of the ordinary until we made him a star! For nine months running, he's been the List's only straight single man living in Greenwich Village. Although he receives more than twenty calls a day, Dr. Weissblatt has not lost his priorities: "I am hard at work on a Water Pik infomercial and seek someone fabulous to share my life with." Dr. Weissblatt is eager to hear from bisexual women.

OLDEST LIVING ENGLISH GRADUATE STUDENT TELLS ALL Bart McBride, 55, has been writing his thesis for thirty years and works the midnight shift at Kinko's on Thirty-third and Lexington Avenue. Bart lives with his mother and has never married. "I am a perfectionist," he explains. "That's why I haven't finished my thesis, or moved." Just waiting for the right girl.

CAMELOT REVISITED Jason Webster, 26, congressional aide. Jason is obsessed with Sarah Jessica Parker and wants to marry an Ivy League graduate who looks just like her. "I know this limits my playing field, so to speak, but I don't want to give any wrong signals. If someone reads this who looks just like Sarah Jessica, went to Brown, and likes Caio Fonseca's paintings, Knopf books, Prada shoes, and water polo, please call me. I want to marry you."

She Saw Through Us

Her cakes have survived the suburbanization of the fifties and the fat-free restraint of the nineties. By the time Martha Entenmann (1906–1996) died at the age of eighty-nine, the family-owned company she helped to build into an empire had been sold several times over, the last time to CPC International as part of an $865 million deal.

The see-through cake box was invented by Martha Entenmann in the same way that Jennie Grossinger built a Catskill resort and Julia Waldbaum created the supermarket bearing her family's name. Of course, I'm slightly exaggerating. But if you're looking for female role models in the fifties, the story of Martha Schneider and her rise from bakery salesgirl to czarina of all the metropolitan strudels was one any girl with a little talent would envy.

Martha married the bakery boss when she was nineteen, then expanded their bread-and-rolls trade into a thriving Long Island home-delivery business. After her husband's death, Mrs. Entenmann and her sons realized they could make their cake and sell it, too. Quality baked goods at the time came in white paper boxes tied up with red strings. Any child or mouse had to gnaw a small hole in the side to get a preview of the best part of dinner. But an Entenmann pie or chocolate doughnut arrived in that see-through box with a proud blue Entenmann banner. Just that hint of homemade heaven caused those Entenmann baked goods to jump off the shelves in supermarkets from Long Island to Miami.

When parents came to visit their children at summer camp, they brought Entenmann's cookies. When college students pulled an all-nighter, they had Entenmann's doughnuts. When familes sat shiva for the dearly departed, they served Entenmann's blackout cake. Entenmann's meant quality goods. Ann Page, Sara Lee, and Betty Crocker had their talents, but Entenmann's, even from the supermarket, was family.

For fifty years, until her retirement fifteen years ago, Mrs. Entenmann took an active role in the family company. This is important to know: Mrs. Entenmann cannot be blamed for the current fascination with "fat-free" baked goods. One wonders if Frank Sinatra would have been quite so obsessed with Entenmann's crumb cake—for years he had them shipped to his home in Palm Springs—if there was absolutely nothing to feel guilty about. Memories of coffee cakes and bundts have much more to do with comfort and pleasure than with abstinence. I like to think Mrs. Entenmann knew that.

Long before there were luncheon panels and seminar weekends devoted to female role models juggling career and domesticity, Mrs. Entenmann helped to run a baking empire and raised a family with nine great-grandchildren. Only someone with that kind of patience, loyalty, and initiative could invent the see-through convertible bakery box top. Martha knew what it took to make it through the night.

First Ladies Get Dressed

Joan Rivers and her daughter, Melissa, follow Hillary Clinton and Elizabeth Dole into their closets.

JOAN: I am standing between two turquoise Dana Buchman suits and I am thrilled! Hillary, can you give us a little preview of what you will be wearing while campaigning this week?

HILLARY: Joan, it takes a wardrobe to make a closet. I wish we could be sitting around a kitchen table and really discussing our fashion hopes and fears. But I know we are both too committed to our families to have that much fun, so let me give you a few highlights.

For the Monday morning Yale Law School Association Alumnae Committee, I'll be wearing that boxy turquoise Dana Buchman suit with Trifari goldlike accessories. When I watch Chelsea doing her homework, I am proud that first ladies never wear real jewelry. For the Tuesday Upper West Side Liberal Democrat Luncheon, I will be wearing this Indian bedspread with silver earrings and Fred Braun sandals that I have saved since 1968. And then, on Thursday night, for the David Geffen Birthday Party in the Lincoln Bedroom, Barbra's best friend Donna made me this Lycra off-the-shoulder dress that my best friend Mary says her husband Ted swears is Tom's wife Rita's favorite look. Joan, I am a very spiritual person, and for the Friday afternoon Coalition of Christians, Jews, and Muslims Tea, I will be wearing this nun's habit, a chador, and a mezuzah pin on my lapel. Finally, for my Saturday walk with the president in the Rose garden, I will be wearing comfortable family-time clothes that I order from catalogues at 3:00 in the morning when I've finished reading what I wore wrong that week.

JOAN: Have you ever ordered from Victoria's Secret?

HILLARY: No. But my husband has.

JOAN: My daughter is standing by, in your opponent's closet. Missy, this has been so exciting!

MELISSA: Mother, I am standing between two Liz Claiborne suits and rows and rows of matching pumps. It's thrilling!

ELIZABETH: God bless you, Melissa. Tonight, I'd like to break tradition and come into the closet with you. Do you mind if I take your microphone? Melissa, every morning when I come into this closet I think to myself, I am choosing this pump for my husband because he was born in a Kansas small town and he knows what it means for every American to put on his shoes in the morning. Melissa, I hope someday you love a man the way I love my husband.

JOAN: I hope so, too.

ELIZABETH: God bless you, Joan. When I get dressed, I remember that my husband may have been poor in material things but was rich in values. And that's what I look for in my clothes—values like honesty, decency, hard work, love of family, and patriotism. For the Monday morning Harvard Law School Association Alumnae Committee, I will be wearing this pumpkin Liz Claiborne suit with matching pumps and Monet costume jewelry. Years ago, my husband told me he would rather feed the hungry than give me jewelry, and I wept. Then, for the Tuesday Daughters of the South Garden Luncheon, I will be wearing this lovely dress that I wore to my first cotillion, in 1954. I hope this dress is a bridge to a past America. For the Thursday night Party at Planet Hollywood, Bruce and Demi have invited a few of their friends to meet us, but we don't expect any of them to come, so I'll be wearing the same Bill Blass I wore to Charlton Heston's birthday party. For the Friday American Red Cross Volunteers Tea, I will be wearing a simple Yves Saint Laurent suit that I bought downstairs in my apartment complex in Washington. So many American working women have time to shop only when it's convenient. For the Saturday Walk with My Husband Along the Potomac, I always wear American blue jeans. My husband is a genuine war hero, and blue jeans are my badge of honor.

JOAN: I am so moved. I am weeping! Melissa, aren't these two remarkable women?

MELISSA: Yes, they are, Mother. I can't wait to see what they'll be wearing to the debate Sunday night. And we'll be there!

THE SUNDAY NIGHT GREAT DEBATE

JOAN: I don't think I've ever seen the first lady looking quite so versatile. Can you explain your choices tonight?

HILLARY: I have chosen Joan & David airwave pumps that the Olympic gymnast Kerri Strug signed when she visited the White House, a turquoise Dana Buchman skirt for good luck, a red Liz Claiborne jacket to show that Democrats can wear middle-of-the-road Republican red, a pin made by the Sausalito teachers' association, and a Donna Karan scarf, because my husband and I are committed to women and American values. I have a velvet bow in my hair because it's fun, and it takes fun to be a first lady.

JOAN: Well, you look wonderful. Back to you, Melissa.

MELISSA: Mother, I don't think I've ever seen Mrs. Dole looking more professional and relaxed. Can you explain your choices tonight?

ELIZABETH: All eyes should really be on my husband tonight. He is my Rock of Gibraltar. I am his support. And to support him I am wearing airwave Joan & David pumps, a turquoise Dana Buchman skirt to show that Republicans can wear waves-of-majesty Democratic purple, a red Liz Claiborne jacket to honor Nancy Reagan, a pin made by the Raleigh transport workers, a Donna Karan scarf to show my support for Israel. Finally, I am wearing this velvet hair bow because my husband and I believe in the greatness of the American individual.

Hillary and Elizabeth enter the auditorium. They see that they are dressed exactly alike, look at their husbands, and embrace.

JOAN: I am weeping! Weeping!

MELISSA: Me, too, Mother!

JOAN: This is a great day for American women!

MELISSA: Mother, do you know what the candidates are wearing?

JOAN: Suits and ties. Don't be so nosy, Melissa.

Good, Better, Bette

I am forty-five minutes late to meet Bette Midler. We are meeting at her loft in Manhattan's Tribeca. It happens to be Gay Pride Day, and the streets of Greenwich Village have been cordoned off by the NYPD for the parade. My taxi is trapped near the Holland Tunnel between Gay Pride commuters from Menlo Park, New Jersey. I keep telling myself that if anyone will understand, it will be Bette, who has been for decades a supporter and icon of the gay community. I can't seem to find her building, which is way unassuming. When I finally arrive, the Divine Miss M greets me at her self-service elevator. She is wearing a silver lamé bikini and emerges on the half shell.

SCENE ONE

BETTE: You're late.

WENDY: You're wearing lamé.

BETTE: I can't find my chandelier.

WENDY: Have you lost it?

BETTE: It makes such a nice hat.

WENDY: But it's Sunday.

BETTE: So?

WENDY: I was just thinking you'd be slightly more informal.

BETTE: I was thinking you'd be more on time.

WENDY: I got stuck behind a parade.

BETTE: Which one?

WENDY: Gay Pride.

BETTE: Then it's all right. Why are you staring at me?

WENDY: You are everything I thought you would be. You are everything everyone thinks you'd be.

BETTE: Yes. I don't like to surprise anyone. I live strictly according to my stereotype. Do you like my song "Friends"?

WENDY: It's wonderful!

BETTE: Good. We'll sing it in the elevator.

Bette closes the elevator door. She hands me the sheet music of "Friends" as the elevator begins playing the familiar tune. We sing together, "You've gotta have friends."

SCENE TWO

Bette Midler's living room, which has at least fifty purple paper lanterns on the ceiling and an expansive view of the Hudson River.

BETTE: I wouldn't live anywhere but downtown. Would you like some Pellegrino water?

WENDY: Sure.

BETTE: Where do you live?

WENDY: Uptown. But I think I should move back downtown.

BETTE: Why don't you do what you want?

WENDY: Because I don't have the confidence you have. Because I would never have the guts to cover my ceiling with purple lanterns. Because you have created a lovable, larger-than-life personality, and I am devoted to making mine smaller and smaller.

BETTE: What are you talking about?

WENDY: Everything we were told we shouldn't do as girls you were brave enough to do.

BETTE: Are you sure you have the right apartment?

WENDY: You're ballsy, sassy, warm, sexy, and—let's face it—you don't have the arms of Gwyneth Paltrow or Michelle Pfeiffer.

BETTE: This is the strangest interview I've ever had.

WENDY: I am obsessed with your confidence!

BETTE: Do you take Prozac? Maybe deep breathing would help. Or a bath.

WENDY: You made every girl like me think maybe it's all right to be ourselves.

BETTE: And that's bad?

WENDY: It's really confusing.

BETTE: Would you like to lie down?

WENDY: Yes.

BETTE: Just curl up on the couch. You'll feel better soon. Maybe it was all that traffic. I'll sing you a lullaby.

Bette begins to sing "The Rose." Wendy falls asleep.

SCENE THREE

Bette Midler's dining room table.

BETTE: Better?

WENDY: Much better.

BETTE: Your eyes are wandering all around the room. Do you want me to give you a tour of my apartment?

WENDY: No, that's fine. I just have an eye that goes out slightly.

BETTE: Oh, there I was thinking you were bored, and really it's an affliction.

WENDY: I'm sorry.

BETTE: Please stop apologizing.

WENDY: There's nothing wrong with my eyes. I'm just curious. That's all.

BETTE: Because you'd like to make some quick assessments.

WENDY: Mention Bette Midler and the expectation is outrageous.

BETTE: Does my domesticity bore you?

WENDY: No, but in truth you seem just like everyone else. A successful working woman.

BETTE: These days I am trying to be a little more relaxed about work. I was never meaner to anyone than myself. Now I hope I've grown up a little and given up the angst. Do you mind if I change out of this half-shell outfit into overalls and a T-shirt? I actually like to be in comfortable clothes.

W E N D Y : But that's so normal!

B E T T E : I know. I'm disappointingly normal. Frankly, my daughter was the best change in my life. Does that sound too much like everyone else? Because for me it's very special. Are you married?

W E N D Y : No.

B E T T E : I thought you were. It's hard work, but worth it.

W E N D Y : I've been thinking that.

B E T T E : And you look great. I like your hair. I say the older you get, the blonder you get.

W E N D Y : I think it would be peculiar if I went any blonder.

B E T T E : You're much too self-conscious. You can be anyone you want to be.

Bette begins to sing "When You Wish upon a Star." Wendy is weeping.

SCENE FOUR

Bette and Wendy with silvery gum wrappers in their hair at the Oribe Salon.

B E T T E : People are a lot less original than they used to be. Personalities used to be so much stronger. I find coolness equals dull.

WENDY: Most people find coolness equals cool.

BETTE: Boring.

WENDY: And withholding equals interesting.

BETTE: Where are you getting this from? You need to have a better time and wear makeup.

WENDY: I never wear makeup.

BETTE: I eat, breathe, and live for makeup.

WENDY: Why?

BETTE: It's fun. You should try it.

WENDY: Other people do it better.

BETTE: Who cares? Don't you work hard enough in life?

WENDY: Yes.

BETTE: So why make the simple things even harder? Just repeat after me, "Anything you can do, I can do better."

Bette sings "Anything You Can Do, I Can Do Better." The entire beauty parlor in pink robes joins in the chorus.

SCENE FIVE

Bette and Wendy at the Saks Fifth Avenue makeup counter.

MAKEUP GIRL: I think you are one of the greatest women of this century.

BETTE: I can think of other greater women. Doctors, environmentalists, teachers, dancers. I really admire dancers. They have such discipline.

MAKEUP GIRL: But you always make me laugh.

BETTE: Comedy is very easy for me. When you know what's funny, you can be funny. I love to laugh. I find it's therapeutic. I love to laugh till I cry. What do you have in a lip liner?

MAKEUP GIRL: I can't believe I'm selling Bette Midler lip liner.

BETTE: It's for my friend Wendy here. She's scared of makeup.

MAKEUP GIRL: That's so sad.

WENDY: I got frightened by a mascara wand when I was six.

BETTE: She thinks only one kind of woman deserves to feel attractive.

MAKEUP GIRL: That's insane.

BETTE: I told her that.

MAKEUP GIRL: It's no big deal.

BETTE: I told her that too. There are much more important things in life. When I turned fifty I did a little stocktaking, and basically, I've done what I set out to do, had fun along the way, and haven't offended too many people. My family is intact. My daughter is a great person. I've been well rewarded. You don't get any credit for being happy. But ultimately I'm positive.

Bette begins to sing "Got the Sun in the Morning and the Moon at Night." Wendy buys one hundred Topaz lip liners.

SCENE SIX

Wendy and Bette in a rowboat on the Hudson River. It is twilight.

WENDY: I love the city at twilight. I can't think of any time that's more romantic.

BETTE: You're a real New Yorker?

WENDY: A nice Jewish girl from Brooklyn.

BETTE: I came to New York in 1965. I'm a nice Jewish girl from Hawaii.

WENDY: Not common.

BETTE: A specialty act. I have always had a sense of not being a mainlander. And when I got here I didn't have the same experience as everyone else. For instance, I never went to college.

WENDY: I first heard about you when I went to Yale.

BETTE: Miss La-di-da.

WENDY: I was at drama school. My friends saw you at the Continental Baths.

BETTE: That was an amazing time.

WENDY: Over twenty years ago. Most women aren't allowed to stick around for such a long time.

BETTE: Could you please row instead of talk?

WENDY: What I mean is, you're a survivor.

BETTE: See that little red lighthouse under the George Washington Bridge? That was cleaned up by the New York Restoration Project. I was part of that. I take a lot of satisfaction now in the world's surviving. Not just me. Maybe that's what turning fifty is all about. Personally, I've never been happier.

Bette sings "Shine On Harvest Moon." Wendy harmonizes and rows.

SCENE SEVEN

The stage at Radio City Music Hall. Wendy rises from the orchestra pit in a lamé bikini on a half shell with a blond wig and six-foot eyelashes.

WENDY: And you were expecting the Little Mermaid? Tonight, I'd like to introduce someone who has taught us all that a woman can be funny, sexy, warm, fifty, a perfectionist, a mother, glitzy, colorful, smart, and confident. I am proud to present my new best friend, Bette Midler.

The Rockettes tap on stage in rose-spangled hot pants, and Bette simply walks out in overalls and a sweatshirt.

BETTE: I want to thank my new best friend, Wendy, and I want everyone to tell her how much they love her lip liner.

ALL OF RADIO CITY: We love your lip liner, Wendy.

Bette and Wendy sing "Together Wherever We Go."

Diary

Sunday in New York. I had plans to spend the day reading
V. S. Naipaul in bed and taking an aerobics class. This
was mostly caused by seeing *Secrets and Lies,* the opening
film at the New York Film Festival. Not that it has anything
to do with V. S. Naipaul, but in the film, a rather centered
woman who plays an optometrist spends her birthday at home
reading.

Overslept Sunday morning. Didn't get around to reading
V. S. Naipaul or the paper, but went to Jane's aerobic class.

Took a cab downtown to have lunch with Nicholas Hytner,
who will be directing a film I wrote based on Stephen
McCauley's *The Object of My Affection: A Novel.* Nick's film of
Arthur Miller's *The Crucible* is coming out in November, and
it's fantastic. Anyway, when I think about a positive trajectory
in my life, it's a Sunday lunch with Nick and this particular
afternoon.

My friend Paul Daniels invited me to see a concert by

Dancers over 40 at the Dance Theater Workshop. We sat behind Louise Roberts, who was the receptionist at the June Taylor School of Dance when I was growing up.

I loved the Dancers over 40. Especially a waltz danced by Stuart Hodes and Alice Teirstein. Hodes was Martha Graham's partner in the 1950s. His face is amazing, and his dancing was elegant and joyous. Nick and I want to cast him in our film. A star is born. Schwab's drugstore at Dancers over 40.

Had dinner with another friend, Peter Schweitzer, a producer at CBS, and his parents. Peter's mother remembers the names of all his former girlfriends. His stepfather was a writer on *Hawaii Five-O.* I am reminded of the dinners I would have with friends of my parents in high school, and wonder what it would be like to have real conversations with them. It's actually a game my sister and I used to play. We'd sit upstairs in synagogue and pick out which ladies we thought we'd like to have as mothers. My sister preferred the intellectuals. I always selected the ones who looked warm and wore purple.

Came home around 1:00 a.m. Haven't worked. Haven't read V. S. Naipaul. Feel a cold coming on and anxiety about deadlines on the way. I make a resolution to work and be calm. I make that resolution every night.

DAY TWO
TUESDAY, OCTOBER 1, 1996

Cold came on as anticipated, accompanied by anxiety, fear, and loathing. Decided I didn't feel well enough to go to Washington as planned. Felt extremely guilty, of course, since it was for a committee I've been on for years.

Tried to work and wrote a piece about Robert Isabell, the events coordinator, for *Elle Decor* magazine. I take assignments because I think they'll take me places I wouldn't ordinarily go. That sounds like an essay for a College Board Advanced Placement Test. I take assignments to avoid my larger issues like my play that is opening this spring. I take assignments because it's nice to get paid.

We're in the middle of casting my new play. Casting Broadway plays can be more difficult than off-Broadway since one needs actors to sign up for extended runs. As television attracts more and more stage actors (David Hyde Pierce and Christine Lahti were both in my play *The Heidi Chronicles*), it gets harder to find people to commit to extended runs. It's frustrating when a lot of the really good people have moved to Los Angeles. Of course, the British theater was always thought to be different, since television, film, and theater are centralized in London. But my playwright friends tell me the same is true there now. Maybe even worse. More West End theaters will be empty this season than on Broadway.

Finished piece for *Elle Decor*. Finished "Diary" entry. Now I can't wait to get back to my play. A friend told me about a painter tonight whom she never sees because she's always working. I know the painter. Her name is Cathy Murphy. I admire her work enormously. I make another note to become more disciplined. Meanwhile, I've filled the day with appointments.

But a girl needs a haircut.

DAY THREE
WEDNESDAY, OCTOBER 2, 1996

Went to see my new apartment. I was supposed to move in around five months ago. I tell myself I could easily live anywhere and never notice the surroundings. I have, in fact, lived in a hotel for the past year. Of course, it's a rather upscale joint. On particularly bad days, I aspire to being a character in *Grand Hotel* who stays in the bridal suite until the last penny runs out. Anyway, I'm sort of excited about moving in, and sort of wish I had the guts to start again in Jerusalem.

Managed to avoid work most of the day. Had a board meeting for the British American Arts Association. Ten years ago, I received a mid-career stimulation grant from them. Now I am advising them on international arts conferences. Jennifer Williams, the artist from Portland, Oregon, who runs this organization, is the best of not-for-profit. She's tireless, committed, hopeful, canny, and altogether impressive. I doubt she notices Bottega Veneta bags.

Sat in a friend's dress shop on Madison Avenue for an hour in the afternoon and watched women try on two-thousand-dollar dresses. I have no idea why I am so riveted by this. I tell myself it's character studies for my next play. I am fascinated by the insularity of the rich. I am appalled by their entitlement.

Actually finished a piece, and will begin work on another tomorrow. Hoping to finish all magazine pieces by Saturday and return to my play. No casting news. I try not to think about it.

Had dinner with a friend whose brother, like mine, just got married. The couples at dinner spoke about their children and their schools. Personally, I was rejected by most private schools in Manhattan. A man on the British American Arts Association board told me about a study that has recently been done proving that baby boomers have, by and large, the same values as their parents. It's the following generation that seems to be emerging with different values.

Thinking of canceling breakfast with my mother tomorrow. She's very eager to tell me my brother's third wife is his best wife. I think I need to work.

DAY FOUR
THURSDAY, OCTOBER 3, 1996

Canceled breakfast with my mother. Promised I would see her tomorrow. We have a habit of having breakfasts together so I can leave for a meeting before the questions become too personal.

Odd keeping a diary. It's odd knowing exactly how time is mismanaged. I am simultaneously keeping a food diary in my five hundredth attempt to manage weight. It seems to me I now have two documents to prove that others are far more disciplined and innately good. I am debating whether to list the french fries on the food-management document or the time I spent on a sofa with my cat thinking about absolutely nothing.

Anyway, in an attempt to know where the time goes, here's an exact schedule of yesterday's events:

8:30   Canceled breakfast with my mother.

9:00–9:45   Wrote "Diary" entry for *Slate*.

9:45–10:00 Returned calls. Spoke to Nick Hytner about our film.

10:30–11:15 Had egg white omelet at Orloff's delicatessen and cut piece for the *Times* style section.

11:15–12:00 Returned calls. Approved piece for *Elle Decor* about Robert Isabell's apartment. Told my friend Henry I couldn't meet him at the museum.

12:00–2:00 First meeting as chair of Program Committee at WNET—our public television station. Sat next to Walter Cronkite. Don't quite understand how I became chairperson since I still feel that in any meeting I should be passing notes to my friends about the teacher's hair. But I genuinely care about public television. Of course, it amazes me that anyone could say they genuinely don't care.

2:00–3:00 Returned more calls. Agreed to do a piece about Kmart opening in New York. Of course, I had just promised myself that I would work only on my play.

3:00–5:00 Returned to my apartment/hotel room with the intention of making a cup of tea and working. Called my sister, and we chatted about her mother-of-the-bride dress. Thought a long time about calling an old boyfriend. Thought it would certainly give the day some texture. Lift it out of the doldrums of work or not work. Called an old friend instead. Decided to take a nap, except I was too nervous. Decided to walk downtown, around two miles, to have dinner with the Red Meat Club.

5:20–6:00 Walked down Madison Avenue in the rain. Very calming despite the traffic lights.

6:00–7:30 Dinner with the Red Meat Club, my friends Heidi and Carole, who meet around every two months for steaks. We generally land up at joints like Morton's, where out-of-town male traders sit in suspenders. Carole is a director, and Heidi a set designer—both are producers. Generally, we are the only theatrical folks at the steak joints. We talked about my casting, Heidi's show in London, and Carole's new theater. Had too many french fries. Won't list them in the food diary.

7:45–9:45 Saw *The First Wives Club*—complicated response. Happy those three women are so good in it. Happy more films about women will be made because this one is making money. But most women I know don't end up having catfights and slapping each other. Interesting that *How to Marry a Million-aire* was a fifties fantasy and *Getting Dumped by a Millionaire* is the nineties version. I could be pretentious and say "Revenge" has been a viable dramatic theme since Jacobean tragedy. But that's neither here nor there. Maybe I wish there were parts for Diane Keaton other than either being dumped or the mother of the bride.

10:30–11:00 Finally began reading V. S. Naipaul. His first trip back to Bombay.

11:00 Lights-out. Early breakfast with Mother tomorrow. Can't cancel. Haven't written a word or called the old boy-friend. Will list the french fries.

DAY FIVE
FRIDAY, OCTOBER 4, 1996

I went to see my mother for breakfast, which was actually fine. She was wearing leather. Well, black leather pants and an *Isn't It Romantic* (an earlier play of mine) T-shirt. She offered me her wedding china for my new apartment and eight silver ice-cream cups for dress-up.

Had coffee with a very nice man who wants to do my children's book for Disney's Sunday night TV show. I remember watching it with my brother—Fantasyland and fireworks. Anyway, it sounds interesting, except I have to write it.

After the french fries debacle, had sushi lunch with my agent. She told me that the bad English notices for my play there included references to the bad notices for my previous play there. I told her I wasn't really interested in reading them, but I'm disappointed, because I'd always secretly planned to live in London half the year.

Came to Boston because I'm speaking on a panel for the International Women's Forum. Was asked to nominate the Woman of the Century and voted for Agnes de Mille. My fellow panelists came up with Margaret Sanger, Eleanor Roosevelt, and Virginia Woolf. Felt slightly embarrassed but secretly pleased. Taking my niece, who is a freshman at Harvard, out to dinner. Pamela is studying moral reasoning and travel writing— both sound so pleasurable. I think I should be in her classes instead of speaking on panels.

Met my college roommate Mary Jane and her fiancé for a drink. I first met Mary Jane when she was Pamela's age. I wonder if Pam can even imagine us as people who shared a dorm room and lit candles to listen to Laura Nyro.

Am very happy about Mary Jane's marriage. Personally, I feel halfway between *Travels with My Aunt* and a girl who first saw Harold Pinter's *The Homecoming* in the Loeb Drama Center basement. I was very impressed. But I didn't know then that Harold Pinter only wears black.

I think my mind is receding. I wonder how long I can coast.

Three Sisters

Playwright's Confession

During the run of *The Sisters Rosensweig* I have often been stopped in ladies' rooms in theaters or at a sample sale with a half-priced item draped halfway over my head and asked, "Are you Wendy? Which sister are you?" Of course, I am always tempted to say that I am not Wendy, I am Kate Moss, the model in the Calvin Klein ads, and furthermore I have no sisters.

Frankly, I don't think a play is really playing if the author has to explain it. Did Chekhov have three sisters? Did George S. Kaufman and Moss Hart want to take it with them? And did Noël Coward have a design for living? I leave such questions to guest deconstructionists on very late-night cable talk shows. All I can say is that *The Sisters Rosensweig* and I owe much to all four playwrights.

For the record, I am the youngest of three sisters, and my oldest sister never dates faux-furriers. My sister Sandra named me after Wendy in *Peter Pan,* and my initial knowledge of the theater was from original cast albums she bought from the Broadway plays we attended. My sister, who at the time seemed to me one of the most sophisticated people alive, except for Loretta Young and Margot Fonteyn, was a theater lover, and her affection and tickets sometimes included me. My other sister, Georgette, and I knew that while we were at home struggling with time-distance problems and the meaning of *Man Without a Country*, girls from our very own dancing school were tapping on Broadway every night. So although my sisters are not necessarily the characters in this play, they are in many ways at the heart of my entire theatrical interest.

Over the years, I have known many actresses whose career opportunities diminished because they made the grievous error of growing older. Therefore I deliberately set out to write smart and funny parts for women over forty. I also created, hopefully, a very nice man who falls in love at first sight with one of them.

This is not an angry play. It is a play of possibilities. My first playwriting teacher told me that there is order in art, not in life. My contention is that life can imitate art if the artists change the accepted variables. Mervyn, the world leader in synthetic animal protective covering, and Sara, the international banker, are not romantic fantasies. They are grown-ups whom we don't get to see on stage often enough.

One issue that hasn't been addressed much about *The Sisters Rosensweig* is that of identity. Geoffrey, the world-class director and one of my favorite people in the play, confesses to his beloved Pfeni, "You don't know what it's like to have absolutely no idea who you are!" Despite their maturity, most of the characters in the play are struggling with who they are. There's a reason why these three sisters are from Brooklyn and the play takes place in Queen Anne's Gate, London.

When the show began to tour, a year after the play opened in New York, I went to see it in Norfolk, Virginia. I had no idea if it would work outside New York, particularly in a town that is known for its naval acumen. As I watched it, I became a little envious of the author. Whoever wrote this play has consistently lucked out with spectacular casts. Clearly, the success of the evening was due in large part to the author's having been in the rehearsal room with every single one of them.

At the end of the evening I thought to myself that this author must be very mature. She must believe in family and personal history. She must believe in the challenge and tradition of well-structured plays. She must believe there are possibilities. Obviously, then, the author could not possibly be me.

Afternoon of a Fan

My feet were too flat for toe shoes. During elementary school I studied ballet with Richard Thomas, the actor's father. My memory for the combinations—*glissade, assemblé, jeté*—was quick and effortless, while my execution was quite the opposite. Happily, I realized at a very young age that my future in dance was not on stage, but growing up as an audience member of the New York City Ballet.

The company was still at the City Center when my sister Sandra first took me to see *Stars and Stripes*. Previously I had thought that ballet was limited to dying swans with fantastic metatarsal arches. I had no idea it could be so energetically charged that the Radio City Spectacular would seem a little dull in comparison. As far as I was concerned, *Stars and Stripes* was thrilling even without a dancing manger.

By the time I was in high school the City Ballet had moved to Lincoln Center and my taste had become slightly more sophisticated. Suzanne Farrell as Dulcinea became my feminine ideal. She was grace, beauty, and a muse, everything a New York City high school girl should aspire to be. As for the masculine ideal, there was my real life—Horace Mann school mixers with boys desperate to get into Yale and faking the twist—and, on the other hand, there was Edward Villella as Apollo.

At that point I was still younger than most of the dancers in the company and took the greatest delight in spotting them in the corps and secretly plotting their ascent. I felt proprietary when those in charge ultimately noticed what I had already discovered in the first-class work of Merrill Ashley and Kyra Nichols. Somehow, from constantly flipping to the cast lists until I figured out the names of all the corps dancers, I knew I was involved. In my mind Heather Watts was my classmate. As the flowers poured on stage for her very touching farewell performance in 1995, I remembered first seeing her name on the company roster. There's a continuity in growing up with the ballet both for the artist and for the audience.

Whenever my parents or my sister took me to the ballet we sat in the orchestra. However, when I was in town from college or graduate school, I chose the graciousness and economy of the fourth ring. Perhaps my greatest seating coup was the afternoon I noticed from my uppermost perch two empty seats, first ring, dead center. After intermission I very nonchalantly discarded my coffee cup and blondie and unobtrusively swept onto my waiting empty prey. As the lights were going down, I was making myself very comfortable when both Mr. Robbins and Mr. Balanchine asked me if I was in the right seat. I didn't stop to tell them how much I admired their work.

My infatuation with the ballet has only grown deeper since I've been writing plays. Perhaps it's because my knowledge is all appreciation. Unlike in the theater, I'm not familiar enough to be critical, or an insider. Moreover, for a dramatist there's an incomparable joy in watching world-class artists create so eloquently in silence. There is no performing art in which content merges so perfectly with form as the ballet. I am constantly reinspired by the structure of *The Four Tempera-ments*, the innovation of *Reliquary*, the simplicity of *Afternoon of a Faun*, and the storytelling of *Don Quixote*.

It's no wonder to me that I am always running into people I know from the theater on the grand tier. The playwright Albert Innaurato's knowledge of ballet is encyclopedic, and Jonathan Alper, the late dramaturg of the Manhattan Theatre Club, could give nightly updates of the cast for every performance. Last season, Nicholas Hytner, the director of *Carousel* and *The Madness of King George,* and I went to an all-Robbins matinee and ran immediately into Tommy Tune and the casting director Joanna Merlin. That Robbins afternoon was perfection, everything I had hoped growing up to have a cultural life in New York would be. The range of the choreographer, from *Glass Pieces* to *Afternoon of a Faun,* was a pure gift to this afternoon audience, and the company was even more energetic than the one I remembered from *Stars and Stripes* thirty years ago. After *West Side Story Suite* Nick and I remained in our seats. It's seldom that a performance will reinforce and revitalize the reason one chose to have a life in the theater. By coincidence, fate, and very good luck, our seats were the same ones I borrowed from Mr. Robbins all those years ago.

Twenty-two ballets are returning to the repertory this season, including my high school flame, *Apollo.* I am now older than all of the members of the company. But I look forward this spring to scanning my program for the twenty new dancers who have recently joined and choosing the ones I know will ascend. I'm anticipating the joy I had when Albert Evans became a principal and noticing this year Edward Liang and Monique Meunier. They are now on my list. This season I'll renew my yearly resolution to have the integrity and discipline of Wendy Whelan, the airy grace of Yvonne Borrée, the abdominal muscles of Peter Boal, the élan of Damian Woetzel, and of course by June I'll be marrying my ideal mate, Jock Soto. He'll be wearing his red shirt from *West Side Story Suite*. I'll be on pointe.

How to Do a Hollywood
Awards Ceremony

A few Golden Globe truths, up front and personal: Sharon Stone's stomach isn't just flat, it's concave; Tom Cruise and Nicole Kidman really, really love each other, as demonstrated by her towering over him in mint green mules while he still holds her hand and looks up adoringly; Tom Hanks may be the nicest man in the world, or at least the nicest man to be nominated for three Golden Globes in a row; and finally, whoever is Jane Seymour's trainer, whoever is the genius who managed to mold her body into a size five Suzie Wong number just seven weeks after she delivered twins, should get the Republican presidential nomination. Clearly this is the person who can lead the nation not into temptation.

The Golden Globes are awarded annually by the Hollywood Foreign Press Association, those intrepid journalists from Leipzig, Singapore, and Cairo who report on Tinseltown for the worldwide market. A number of years ago this estimable group took a lot of flak for naming Pia Zadora Most Promising Newcomer. This year it has emerged as the Iowa Caucus of awards shows—in other words, as the Golden Globes go, so might go the Oscars. Moreover, it's Hollywood's only awards mixer, combining the very separate worlds of television and feature films. Generally, that oil and water do not mix. Once you've moved up from being a Flying Nun, Mork, or a resident of 90210 to major motion pictures, you seldom go backward. But at the Golden Globes, Sean Connery is in the same ballroom as the cast of *Friends*.

So how did I, a New York playwright, get a chance to mingle with Clint Eastwood and the *ER* team? The Turner Network Television version of my play *The Heidi Chronicles* was the happy recipient of three Golden Globe nominations: Jamie Lee Curtis for best actress in a TV movie, Tom Hulce for best supporting actor, and one nomination for the entire shebang. I first heard about our honors from Tom Hulce, who sang on my phone machine, "And there's one for you and one for me and one for our pal Jamie Lee!" Michael Brandman, the producer, called to tell me the folks at Turner would very generously fly me out West for the festivities, and finally, a congratulatory telegram arrived from Ted Turner himself. I knew chances were we wouldn't win anything, but at least my life was now inextricably tied to Jane Fonda and the Atlanta Braves. I had to be there.

There are two ways to prepare for a Hollywood awards gala: take them seriously or pretend to not take them seriously while all the time taking them dead seriously. As an East Coast writer I took them very seriously indeed, since I am of course acquainted with important intellectual journals such as *People, Us,* and the *Star* and am therefore deeply concerned about Sharon Stone favoring Vera Wang over Valentino. I had my fingers crossed that Emma Thompson, Jodie Foster, and Annette Bening wouldn't appear in matching Armanis (which, by the way, happened that very Golden Globe night. Annette and Sally Field appeared in sister slips with signature Armani spiderwebs on the back. Annette's was black and

Sally's was burnt orange. In fact, aside from the color, Sally's may well have been the more startling because, perhaps as a result of her years as that aerial novice, she has truly defied gravity. Nothing on Sally sags. Of course, nothing on Annette sags either. But Annette wasn't Gidget).

I knew I would emerge a fashion victim or even a suicide if I entered the evening-wear competition. My dressing choices seemed clear: keep it understated, practically unnoticeable, and in no way embarrassing. I opted, therefore, for a black Empire number I purchased three years ago—a little hip and a little hide-the-hips. For that touch of Hollywood glamour, I added a velvet shawl from Barneys sent to me as a gift for the occasion by Iris Grossman, the talented casting director at Turner. Here's a major difference between filmdom and Broadway: in Hollywood you get valuable gifts, on the stage you get flowers. If only we had won—I was hoping for a Land Rover.

I arranged for a lovely woman to arrive at my hotel to do hair and makeup. She told me everyone from her company was busy doing faces for the Globes. I imagined every room at the Four Seasons Hotel, the Peninsula, and the Beverly Hills filled with women staring at their faces and wondering if it's time to call the nice doctor from the "You Can Look Years Younger" ads in the back of *Los Angeles* magazine. Of course, every time I've had makeup done I thank the artist profusely, and then as soon as she's out the door I run into the bathroom to wash it all off. This time I split the difference. I kept all the eye stuff and scrubbed off the vampire lips and the cast-of-*Friends* brows. With a flip of my wrist, I unwrapped my French twist. It's one thing for Gwyneth Paltrow to carry off a croissant in the back of her head, but for me it was a little constraining.

Tom Hulce, my handsome and talented date, arrived with turkey sandwiches and our friend Doug Hamilton, a former

60 *Minutes* producer, in tow. Tom knows the awards ropes from his tour as Mozart in *Amadeus*. Here are the Hollywood awards arrival rules, according to Tom. The later the arrival, the more important the entrance. Always bring a snack, because the wait in the car can take forever. Finally, be sure to meet your driver in a mutually agreed-upon, acceptable position away from the hoopla or it will take forever to make an exit.

Nobody arrives for a Hollywood occasion in a Camry. The lines of limos swept around the block. As we exited the car, at least two hundred photographers popped out to see if we were anybody. Quickly they ascertained that the only one among us who was anyone was Tom. The feeding frenzy, however, was satisfied as Fran Drescher arrived with a vaseful of flowers on her head. "Say it with Fran" made the paparazzi pop.

The Golden Globes is a catered affair; first a champagne supper and then the awards ceremony. The seating, however, is very specific. Movie stars and studio executives are dead center; television is relegated to the second tier. Even movie stars in TV movies, like our Jamie Lee Curtis or Gary Sinise (who appeared as Harry S. Truman for HBO), were demoted that night to the balcony.

Jamie Lee and her daughter Annie arrived, resplendent in Pamela Dennis creations. Sharon Lawrence of *NYPD Blue* had not even one sequin ripple in her long, golden, hugging dress. I resolved never to eat another roll as long as I lived. My eyes then turned to Jessica Lange, one of the few women who appeared real and not bionic, just beautiful. But she pushed her food around the plate and had only a sip or two of champagne. I resolved not only never to eat a roll but also never to swallow anything again.

"Ladies and gentlemen, it's twenty minutes to showtime.

Please take your seats" was announced over the intercom. Now I noticed that the Hulce theory of entrance politics is not only correct but rigorously planned. At fifteen minutes to show-time, Patrick Swayze and Brad Pitt arrived; at ten minutes, Sean Connery and Clint Eastwood; and at five minutes, War-ren Beatty and Annette Bening. Finally, ten minutes after showtime, Michael Eisner, the chairman of Disney, arrived. As I looked around the room at the hundred most familiar faces in the world, I frankly wondered why they bothered to show up. My friend Pat Quinn, an agent at Metropolitan Talent, explained to me that the foreign market is big business and that winning a Golden Globe can turn an American show or movie into a Singapore hit. To be more exact, there's a reason Sylvester Stallone and Sharon Stone are paid the price of the entire National Endowment budget for theater to make one movie.

We lost our first award toward the beginning of the night. Donald Sutherland was named best supporting actor, over Tom Hulce. My defeated date turned to me and whispered, "This is the first award Sutherland has won; I'm happy for him." While I don't want to rip Donald's eyes out, I do think it's no wonder Hulce is considered an actor's actor. During the course of the evening "everybody" cames up to pay homage to my date. "Wendy, you know Tom Hanks," my date introduces us. "And Tom, you know Wendy Wasserstein." Mr. Hanks smiles, "Of course."

Jamie Lee lost to Jessica Lange, and when our nomination for Best TV movie was announced, there was no groundswell of enthusiasm. I was hoping for hoots and hollers and "Way to go, Wendys" from Clint. But I noticed respectful applause from the Sarandon/Robbins contingent, and I hoped they would win every Globe they are ever nominated for.

We lost again to a very good movie about a serial killer in Russia. But I took heart in realizing that my new best friend, Tom Hanks, and the entire *Apollo 13* table, just a few feet below us in the feature-film section, were also shunned. The fact that it grossed more than $472 million seemed momentarily irrelevant. The thing about awards shows is that even commercial winners can be made to feel like losers in front of 100 million viewers worldwide.

The winner who swept the room was Babe the pig. A surge of cheers went up when Jane Seymour showed her legs, along with whispers of "it must have been a surrogate mother." Most intimate moment: Elisabeth Shue's husband wept when she didn't win and she cheered him up. Most verbally proficient acceptance speech: Emma Thompson's (done in the voice of Jane Austen) for her screenplay *Sense and Sensibility*. Finally, the busiest people of the night were the agents, who buzzed from table to table, securing their status with present clients and establishing their presence for new ones.

As I looked out at that room of defined arms, Armani suits, and perfectly untrained goatees, I felt that I had never cracked this town. So I resolved to move, to get much more excited about *Braveheart,* and to review the early work of Courteney Cox. Only then would I not feel this distance. Only then would I have the enthusiasm of an *Entertainment Tonight* reporter.

Leaving with my Golden Globe T-shirt and free samples of Yves Saint Laurent Opium in hand, I found myself trailing Sean Connery on the red carpet. Chris O'Donnell stopped Tom Hulce, of course, to introduce him to his girlfriend, and for a moment the distance was gone. Everyone seemed very familiar; we were dinner companions—James Bond, the Boy Wonder, and me. But as soon as we stepped off that magic carpet,

Tinseltown was intact again. Hollywood is a place where access to Sean, Clint, and Sally is protected by layers of producers, agents, trainers, personal assistants, and even the foreign press. The harder it is to crack, the more glamorous it becomes.

So the next time I go to an awards show, I'm arriving with a bonsai on my head.

Don't Tell Mother

had a temperature of 104 and tonsillitis at my oldest sister Sandra's first wedding. I was six years old at the time, which made her nineteen. My mother tells me that all I wanted was to get out of bed and put on my pearls and white gloves. In fact, my mother repeats this story whenever she feels that I no longer accessorize enough. All I remember from the entire nuptials, which took place in our home in Brooklyn, a sizable red brick corner Dutch Colonial, was my older siblings, Bruce and Georgette, racing upstairs into my sickroom to let me know that Cousin So-and-so had just fallen through the floor while freely interpreting the hora.

My sister Sandra—known to the world as Sandra, never Sandy, from the day she left the Flatbush Dutch Colonial—has always preferred that I not dwell on the wedding story. Frankly, my older sister prefers not to dwell on Brooklyn, our parents, anyone's former marriages, or anything personal, including health and religion—and especially not the cousin who fell through the floor. (I never saw the hole, I never heard of any broken limbs, but I still choose to believe the story.) Even now, Sandra, from behind her desk at the penthouse offices of Clark & Weinstock, management consultants, advises, "If you really want to talk about me as a serious person, you have to think about how that story sounds and looks."

It would be impossible not to talk about my sister as a serious person. She started college at sixteen and graduated with honors at nineteen. Over the course of three decades in mainstream—or, as she prefers, "blue-chip"—corporate America, Sandra was the first female product-group manager at General Foods, in 1969; the first female president of a division of American Express, in 1980; and the first female to run corporate affairs as a senior officer at Citicorp, in 1989. In other words, she never had the luxury of not demanding to be taken seriously.

Two years after her first marriage, Sandra disappeared from my life: she moved to London. She was twenty-one and separated, and she began a career in advertising at the London Press Exchange. For me, "Sandra in London," and even the very tasteful name of Meyer she'd acquired from her husband, became a mythical, glamorous alternative to the bouffant-hair-sprayed mothers at the parent-teacher association, and even to our own mother, Lola, the Polish-born dancer, predestined to plié while broiling lamb chops in Brooklyn. I bragged to the girls' baseball team that my big sister in Europe wrote the "little dab will do ya" Brylcreem jingle. Later, of course, I found out that she was actually an account executive, but it all certainly seemed far more desirable than growing up to chaperon the school trip to the Horowitz Margareten matzo factory.

Around the time that Sandra returned permanently from London, my family moved from Brooklyn to the Upper East Side. When I was in high school, she had a career-gal pad in the East Fifties and was commuting daily to General Foods, in White Plains. Shortly after the Civil Rights Act, the corporate food giant hired the first female associate product manager/

Postum and Toast 'em Pop Ups—my sister Sandra. Our family had cases of unopened Toast 'ems in the kitchen cabinets, and Sandra Meyer moved up to marketing manager/Maxwell House. In that position, she was in charge of the Maxwell House–Folgers coffee wars.

As far as I was concerned, my oldest sister personally sent Tang to the moon and plumped every raisin in Post Raisin Bran. When I visited her in her ever larger offices, she was always the only woman along her corridor who wasn't sitting outside an office glued behind a typewriter and a telephone. Very grown-up, very Darien-looking men named Ed, Rick, and Jim were always popping in and out. Somehow, the love-ins of the late sixties seemed to be eluding them. I always politely shook the gentlemen's hands and couldn't wait for them to leave so I could talk to my sister some more about my prospects at the Horace Mann prom, which were surely more interesting than the marketing potential of Brim.

My mother often asked me if I thought Sandra would marry one of these Eds, Ricks, or Jims. I remember dinners at places like Le Pavillon with my parents, Bruce, Georgette, myself, and Sandra accompanied by various General Foods suits. Afterward, Lola would press me to determine whether the fella meant anything special to her eldest daughter. I never told her that I personally loved it that Sandra was single—partly because I knew those inspection dinners would stop as soon as she married again. I also never told her that my big sister advised me while I was still in high school to stay single until I was thirty unless I fell madly in love. Sex was one thing, and marriage was another, she said.

Sandra finally married the handsomest man who came to dinner, a Robert Redford look-alike. When she gave birth to her first daughter, Jenifer, there was mandatory unpaid maternity leave at General Foods. Therefore, my sister hid her preg-

nancy until her next promotion was confirmed. Her efficiency
in life management, however, never undermined her maternal
commitment. In fact, if you asked my mother, the domestic dancer, and my oldest sister, the corporate player, what
was the most important thing they'd done with their lives,
they'd both say, "Having children." However, my mother
would say the answer was obvious, because "there's no children
like my children," which I always thought should have been
sung by Ethel Merman, while Sandra would clip, "Jenifer and
Samantha are such capable and independent women."

I wish that my sister would tell me what toll her life has
taken on her. Rather, I wish I could get an illogical, nonposi-
tioned answer. But I suppose it's no different than when I'm
asked if I think of myself as a woman playwright. Frankly,
there's really no discussion in either case. My sister would say
that life takes its toll, male or female, period. I heartily dis-
agree. I can't help but wonder what difference it would have
made in my sister's personal or corporate life if she had been a
man. Of course, Sandra would say that if you're a player, gender shouldn't be an issue. But for my generation, gender *is* the
issue.

After my sister's second marriage dissolved, she went to
American Express as vice president, worldwide card product
marketing. In my mind, she and Lou Gerstner, now the chairman of IBM, spent lunches at the Four Seasons devising new
uses for the gold card. At that time, my sister fell madly in
love—the sort of love she advised me to wait for—with
Andrew Kershaw, then the chairman of Ogilvy & Mather,
North America. Andrew died in her house in Pound Ridge six
weeks before the wedding. I waited with Sandra in her Madison Avenue apartment while lawyers arrived to take the paintings he'd brought with him back to his first wife, in Toronto.
Like a good baby sister, I remained in the background for the

entire event. I wanted to take care of her without her knowing
what I was doing. My sister and I stay within our defined
boundaries. She's capable. I'm funny. Except for when I'm sur-
prisingly capable and she's inexplicably funny.

Our mother referred to Sandra when we were growing up as
"Strazac," which means "fireman," but which Mother, for reasons of her own, translated as "a general in the Polish army."
Even as a child, Sandra liked to be in charge. For the record, I
was called Epidemic, because I was always hanging around
and was impossible to send off to bed. Georgette was known as
Gorgeous, for the obvious reasons, and Bruce remained Bruce.
When I look at pictures of Sandra from college, I see a rather
delicate-looking young American girl with beaming brown
eyes and lovely tapered hands. No one would mistake her for a
Polish general, but, of course, I'm not often confused with
black cholera or influenza, either. A few years ago, when Sandra was a senior corporate officer at Citibank, she broke her
leg, and a day after surgery, when a nurse came into her hospital room to change her IV, Sandra snapped at her, "Can't you
see I'm busy? I'm on a business call!" This sort of will is
beyond any *strazac,* or Poland would never have divided. This
sort of determination, I'm sure, is responsible for a very well-
placed corporate lawyer's telling me that my sister saved John
Reed's job at Citibank during its financial crisis. John Reed
is—"of course," as my sister would say—the chairman. What
my sister won't discuss is why so many of her male corporate
contemporaries have become chairmen and she has not. My
sister is a strong woman but not an angry one. Ultimately,
she's a team player.

My favorite Sandra story is another one she would prefer I
not tell. Sandra came home twice from Europe during her five
years away. During one of those visits, I was a third grader at
the Yeshiva Flatbush. (I feel Sandra already blushing.) Every

Saturday, I took dancing classes in Manhattan rather than attend temple services. In order for Sandra and me to get to know each other, my mother suggested that Sandra pick me up from school and take me to Howard Johnson's for a grilled cheese sandwich and on to Radio City for the stage spectacular and a Doris Day film.

My phantom neo-British sister in her gray flannel suit arrived at the dancing school, immediately warned me "Don't tell Mother," and hustled me off to the House of Chan for spareribs and shrimp with lobster sauce. Neither dish was on the rabbi's recommended dietary list at the yeshiva. I was terrified that a burning bush or two stone tablets would come hurtling through the House of Chan's window. But I was with my glamorous big sister, who everyone told me was so brilliant, so I cleaned my plate.

After lunch, we skipped Radio City; Sandra had no interest in the Rockettes or Doris Day. We went to the Sutton Theatre, on East Fifty-seventh Street, which seemed to me the ultimate in style: they served demitasse in the lobby. The feature film was *Expresso Bongo,* starring Laurence Harvey as Cliff Richard's tawdry musical agent. All I remember is a number in a strip joint with girls dancing in minikilts and no tops. I knew that in whatever Doris Day movie we were meant to be going to she would be wearing a top.

I never told my mother, but I loved everything about that afternoon. My big sister Sandra showed me that women, especially a female general with an epidemic, could go anywhere.

Wendy's Workshop

The holidays at our house are a time for family, sharing, and warm celebration. But it only happens through careful preparation. I begin planning on January 2, when I cut off all the amaryllis blossoms in the house and lock them in the bathtub. The door remains sealed until Christmas Eve, when I discover a tubful of blooming trumpets.

Frankly, I want to slap the hand of anyone who thinks nothing can be done with used votive candles. My family uses them as shoe trees until the holidays roll around, when we put one on every step. Last Christmas, we had such a laugh when I accidentally burned my Manolo Blahnik pumps.

Yes, at our house we go all-out for Santa, wrapping the apartment in a red-and-green-flocked wallpaper, just like that talented artist Christo. And it's so easy. Anyone can flock their own paper with confectioners' sugar, spray paint, and glue. I like to use a hair dryer for smoothing out the surfaces. (During the holidays I always carry around a mini.)

Lights, lights, lights. Artichoke lights can give any room that cozy Mediterranean spirit. Just remove the heart with a corkscrew and the unwanted leaves with a tweezer. Dip the artichokes in cloves, vodka, and Carolina Herrera for Men and

let them marinate in the refrigerator for at least five hours.
When the vegetables are firm, string white lights through the
center with No. 5 knitting needles. My mother, Lola, says artichokes give any woman a younger, greener glow.

Holidays are a time for family traditions. Every year I start
the meal with a dreidel full of mango sorbet. Our main course
is always a turkey stuffed with herring, which is very simple to
make as long as the herring is fresh. (The day before Christmas
I fly to Jackson Hole and do my own ice fishing.) And this year
I am inaugurating a new tradition—Kwanza pudding with
Prince Albert's favorite hard sauce.

But it's not the food or the decorating that makes this such
a special season. It's the love we all share. Let me share my love
and holiday pointers with you at: Neiman Marcus, North
Pole; Santa's Rodeo Workshop, Beverly Hills; Wendy's Christmas Living in the Wales Shop, Harrods, where I will be making personal appearances this month. Or write me at Wendy's
Holiday Living. Our e-mail address is wndy@holy.

The Holiday Chronicles

Here's a really great holiday vacation. The day after Christmas I get out my suitcase, stuff it with a sweatshirt for a daytime look, a cashmere cardigan for nighttime glamour—both of these definitely oversized, preferably enormous—add flannel nightgown, and head for a deserted, unfamiliar college town.

I check in advance that the good local innkeeper can provide me with an IBM Selectric typewriter. Of course I know I should really use my Powerbook and coordinated Word-Perfect, ScriptBetter, PlayDoctor, and PlotPositive software. Buy hey, I'm having myself a merry little Christmas and I get to be as cyberstupid as possible. If I want to hand-feed a machine with erasable typing paper, it's my process and I'm welcome to it.

Generally, I arrive after lunch. After check-in, I quickly unpack and move the furniture around so the typewriter has an inspirational view of a pseudo-Oxford gargoyle, a library, or at the very least an evergreen. Finally, I place the-manuscript-I've-deliberately-isolated-myself-to-complete on the desk and flee. After all, no one can write without Ricola sugar-free cough drops. Just ask Joseph Conrad.

Empty streets are festooned with Dickensian decor. Ye Olde Campus Bookstore carries every Christmas cat calendar published; the Republican Women's Cat Calendar, the Gay/ Lesbian Cat Calendar, and the Environmental Cat Calendar. I gather my necessities and spend twenty minutes debating the purchase of a ten-dollar, locally made pottery mug. Finally, I decide I don't deserve it until later in the week, when I've completed my mission. Before returning to my room, I stop in at the local all-natural pizza, pasta, and yogurt parlor for the tallest nonfat extra-foam decaf cappuccino east of Seattle.

Once back, I finally face my manuscript and make my first observation. A holiday trip is no place to start work. One's mind drifts too easily to family, friends, Prozac, and *It's a Wonderful Life.* But New Year's Day is the best possible deadline for the somewhat stalled and uncompleted. Before leaving town it's a swell idea to call an editor or producer and promise them something tangible January first. It certainly solves the entire "What to do on New Year's Eve" dilemma. (The playwright Terrence McNally and I were once on our way to a New Year's Eve party when the anxiety of mutual deadlines overcame us. By midnight we were typing in separate rooms, he in black tie and I in pearls and blue velvet.)

Confronting the semiexistent play, the pulse rises. Will it be possible to ever finish? Is it worthwhile enough to finish? To relieve the uncertainty, an hour call to a friend vacationing in Neva or Saint Grappa, an island only known to platinum American Express card owners, is an absolute necessity. By the end of the call it's at least cocktail hour and time to make the Scarlett O'Hara pledge, "Tomorrow is another day."

A simple rule for holiday writers: Cocktail time is time for physical fitness. Since the purpose of the trip is to work, it's best not to set relaxing precedents. Hollywood screenwriters may at sunset innately desire to bench-press with inspirational music playing in the background, but those of us with at least three fewer zeros after our names would always choose a martini instead. Best to fight the inclination. Best to go for a run on an unlit back road chased by barking dogs to a place you don't know. Orion, on an early-winter night, is spiritually and artistically inspirational. Orion on an early-winter night with wet shoes, frozen hands, no one to talk to is reason enough to go home, have a drink, and start writing.

Ken Ludwig, the Washington author of the current Broadway play *Moon over Buffalo,* told me during rehearsals this fall that the problem with being on the road is "having dinner alone." Dinner is a time to sit beside tomorrow's intended workload, ignore it, and listen carefully to all the surrounding conversation. It's time to judge harshly the surrounding couples in L. L. Bean turtlenecks and duck boots and fantasize about their sex lives. Do they leave the duck boots on? And, of course, it's time to mislead the very pleasant law student/ waiter into thinking you've landed in this place as a cross between Blanche Dubois and Dolores Claiborne.

Since this is a working retreat, late-night entertainment is simply out of the question. After dinner a brief diversion to the message desk is sufficient, and then up to the room. As for television, best to remote-control John Sununu's holiday greeting and the private party girls at 1-900-BE-MERRY in favor of revisiting classics. For instance, I suggest dipping into *The Shoemaker's Holiday,* Thomas Dekker's 1600 Elizabethan comedy, and a sure lights-out in under five minutes.

Next morning the serious work begins. No more excuses, no more excursions. The still unopened manuscript is cracked, the seat at the typewriter is occupied, the power button is turned on. Retyping the last scene to get back in the groove is not as hideous as anticipated. The work is not totally unsalvageable. It's even decent. Of course, it's entirely possible a ghostwriting elf popped into the holiday writer's hotel.

The next week is spent in an obsessive haze of writing, rewriting; a chicken sandwich in the room, another walk stopped midway by barking dogs, another "I have always depended on the kindness of stangers" dinner, and another scene of *Shoemaker's Holiday* before bed. If I were a man, I wouldn't shave both for the Hemingway effect and to avoid the hassle. Since I'm a woman, by the fifth day I hardly dress.

All week I promise myself a movie on Thursday night. But as with Moscow for the three Chekhovian sisters, I know I'll never get there. By Thursday I decide I hate whatever it is I've written, that I've lost my talent, and furthermore I begin inventing my worst-nightmare notices. I get into bed with a case of diet Coke and watch QVC until four o'clock in the morning. I get to sleep only when I am the happy owner of twin $64 ruby rings.

By morning I know it's time to force myself outside. I even put on mascara for the occasion. I take myself to the campus library and hope I will be influenced by the communal concentration. Leaving the room, I leave behind my fear and am able to focus again. I'm back on track. Life will be bliss when I put these pages in an envelope and they are out of my sole possession.

Now my work and I are one. I am not for one moment self-flagellating or lonely. On the contrary, I have a company of characters who are leading me to their final destinations. Of course, since I write plays, our journey together will not be over when I finish the script; most likely it will last another two years. These characters and I will be together for casting, previews, rewrites, and hopefully we will still like each other by opening night. They are my responsibility and my undoing—they are my alternative family. After all, we're spending the holidays together.

I plan to celebrate the night I finish, but I never do. Instead, I arrive at dinner with my completed work and begin to cut, mangle, and torture it until it is legible only to me and a kindergarten class of the very alternatively gifted. As the waiter brings me a final dessert—on writer's holiday, calories, cholesterol, and nicotine are freebies—he asks me if I've had a nice stay.

"Yes," I smile at him, and I think now I've merged with Maggie Smith in *The Prime of Miss Jean Brodie,* "I've had a wonderful time. Happy New Year!"

Looking back at my plays, I remember an inn or hotel room associated with each one. At some crucial point I took myself to the Hanover Inn, Hanover, New Hampshire; the Inn at the Market, Seattle, Washington; the Old Parsonage Inn, Oxford, England; the Duke Diet and Fitness Program, Durham, North Carolina; and my all-time favorite, the Savoy Hotel, London. There's nothing like finishing a play overlooking the Thames and the flashing lights of the Royal National Theatre. It's a honeymoon.

In the middle of these holiday excursions, my mind wanders to what an odd life writing is. Wouldn't it be far healthier to spend the week in the company of real, not imagined, family and friends? I make a plan to integrate my life next year. Set scheduled time for work, personal life, and harpsichord lessons. Then time passes. Unfinished work accumulates. The phone keeps ringing, and I plan my next writing-woman's holiday.

My Low-Fat Dinner
with Jamie Lee Curtis

All I knew about Jamie Lee Curtis before I met her was that she had the best body in the business. The other thing I knew was that her parents were Tony Curtis and Janet Leigh. My parents took me to the movies to watch Tony Curtis and Janet Leigh. We especially liked him because he was born Bernard Schwartz, and my father was born Morris Wasserstein. However, my father has retained his name and never got to wear a dress with Jack Lemmon and join an all-girls band with Marilyn Monroe. Happily, my mother, Lola, never got stabbed in a motel shower by Anthony Perkins.

Rumor has always been that Jamie Lee is "a cool lady." Rumor has also always been that Jamie Lee is very smart. Perhaps the greatest joy of meeting Jamie Lee Curtis is that all of those rumors are true.

Jamie Lee and I did not get off on the right foot. We met for our first lunch at the Four Seasons Hotel in Beverly Hills September of last year. I had been obliquely informed by Turner Pictures that they would produce my play *The Heidi Chronicles* if we cast Jamie Lee Curtis. The fact that the play won the Tony Award and the Pulitzer Prize was not incentive enough for a "go project," but Curtis was. She had just had "a very big year" costarring with Arnold Schwarzenegger in *True Lies*. Jamie was white-hot.

Frankly, I could live perfectly happily ever after if my play never came to television. I wanted to meet Jamie Lee before I said yes.

To say the least, it was a forced luncheon. I arrived jet-lagged and, frankly, a little pissed off at my lack of clout. I made pleasant conversation with Daniel Sullivan, the play director, and Michael Brandman, the TV producer, who was hoping this would all work out so he could get the cameras rolling.

Jamie Lee arrived absolutely on time. Later I learned that Jamie always arrives absolutely on time. She is one of those energized perfectionists.

"Do you want something to eat?" the producer asked her.

"I don't eat," she answered flatly.

OK, I thought, I hate her. She can't do my show. She doesn't eat. She was wearing black jeans and a black turtleneck. She looked taut and scary.

"Have some fruit," the producer insisted.

"OK." She flashed her teeth.

I began staring at her. Jamie Lee is not a woman who immediately radiates vulnerability. She is on the surface a cool, confident number. She is guarded in the way women who have the self-assurance to make the flip, hip remark have taught themselves to be. I am by nature deeply suspicious of that kind of self-assurance because it is not my native habitat.

The fruit plate arrived. She ate one sliver of pineapple.

"We're so excited you want to do *The Heidi Chronicles*." The producer, like all good producers, was the eternal optimist. This meeting would be great and the show would be great.

"I thought I was here for *The Sisters Rosensweig*. My agent told me I was here for the part of the lead, Pfeni. My agent is going to hear from me after this," she said pointedly. "You know I loved *The Sisters Rosensweig*. My friend Richard Frank was great in it."

"Have you ever done a play?" I asked politely.

"No," she answered.

"It's funny—when we were doing the play, Daniel Swee, the casting director at Lincoln Center, always thought you'd be great for the part of Susan in *The Heidi Chronicles*. We even thought of contacting you," I said.

Here's rule number one when dealing with actors: You don't tell a leading lady, especially a very hardworking leading lady who has struggled to earn that status, that you really think she should be in a supporting role.

After my helpful comment, Jamie Lee and I had nothing much more to say. She chatted a bit to the gentlemen, shook all our hands in that cool, confident manner, and left with a final "If I do this, it has to be in the fall because I have another commitment starting in January."

Sullivan urged me to give her the part. "She's very smart. She can do this."

"OK. OK. I think it's 'cause you're a man. But OK. OK." My heart was pounding, my hands were trembling. How was this cool, confident Hollywood number ever going to deliver my sensitive art historian who feels stranded? But OK, OK.

We offered her the part. She turned it down. She believed I didn't like her.

And this, of course, was exactly when I began to really fall for Jamie Lee. She could read me. She knew what she was projecting and she knew what I was fearing.

I wrote Jamie Lee a note apologizing for my behavior on my pink nice-girl stationery. She wrote me back on a very cool,

tasteful pearl-gray: "I want you to be very proud of my Heidi.
That is the most important thing to me."

As an actress Jamie is an extraordinary combination of star
and team player. She knew the names of all the crew, brought
the entire cast coffee, and, most impressive, she paid attention
to every detail of our effort. Jamie Lee could run a studio. She
knows shots, she knows costumes, she knows camera angles.
Jamie Lee is a Hollywood baby.

The Heidi Chronicles follows one woman's journey from 1965
to the present and her involvement in the women's movement.
Jamie Lee is thirty-six, and when she came of age a woman's
right to complete self-definition was already, remarkably, a
given. One night after rehearsal I came back to my hotel room
and waiting for me was a small gift bag from Prada. Attached
to the Prada gift bag was a note: "Thank you for teaching me
how hard it was to get where we are now." The cool, confident
actress and the suspicious playwright now had the beginnings
of a mutual point of view. We shared a common goal: to present a woman with dignity.

We shot for four weeks in Los Angeles. I flew back and
forth from Manhattan because I wanted to be there for *Heidi*
and Jamie. On the final day of shooting, she wept. "This was
the best experience I've ever had." When I look back on it
I think maybe it was because Jamie got to show that she
was more than the best body, a really cool lady, and the daughter of Hollywood royalty. Jamie Lee is a first-rate dramatic
actress.

After *Heidi*, Jamie made three movies back-to-back. I saw
her sporadically. She had dinner for members of our cast at the
Los Angeles home she shares with her husband, Christopher
Guest, the actor, director, and writer, and their eight-year-old
daughter, Annie. Guest is a wryly intelligent man, a star of

This Is Spinal Tap, and a former *National Lampoon*er. Their home is warm and glamorous, and over the living room center wall is a large abstract oil painting with the signature "Tony Curtis."

Dinner chez Guest was a casual event, but the effort was hardly casual. The platters of pasta and mozzarella with basil were perfect. Jamie sat on the edge of the couch, anxious that every guest be happy and content. You wanted to whisper to her, "Relax, you don't have to do everything right." At home, Jamie was very warm, and she put her arms around the guests. She also nibbled. Actually, this is the secret to the best body in the business. Jamie is a nibbler.

Maybe it's that pressure "to do everything right" that makes Jamie talk about "getting out of the business" or "retiring by forty." Jamie and Guest have a home in Idaho, where she sometimes alludes to moving to permanently. "Look, I know this is a young woman's business," she confided to me at a lunch in New York with one of her best friends, Lisa Birnbach. "And I know I'm not some great actress like Meryl Streep. So when it's time to go, I want to have a real life set up." Interestingly, the closer Jamie gets to forty, the more textured her acting has become.

I visited Jamie Lee in London last summer. She was shooting *Fierce Creatures* (a sequel to *A Fish Called Wanda*), and she sent her car and driver to fetch me for the hour drive to Pinewood Studios.

As we walked to a lovely umbrella-shaded table on the movie lot, she happily informed me that she had ordered in advance.

"They've even got my favorite low-fat dressing," she confided joyously. Kevin Kline, Jamie's *Creatures* costar, joined us for lunch. Kevin had recently completed *French Kiss,* and the two actors spoke with insiders' ease about filmmaking in France versus London.

"Do you mind if we take a picture of you?" two zookeepers from the set said as they stopped by our table. (An entire zoo with real and motorized tigers had been constructed by the studio for the film.)

"After lunch." Jamie smiled just enough for them to go away and then turned to Kline and said, "Let me be the bitch, right?"

After Kline left, Jamie told me, "Yesterday Princess Diana stopped by to see me. She was here to visit Tom Cruise." Jamie giggled. "And I wasn't on the set. They had to tell her I was in the loo." Now I had a clearer picture of how her life differs from mine. When I'm in the loo I am seldom keeping royalty waiting.

The following week we met for lunch on the fifth floor of Harvey Nichols, a London department store. It's a chichi spot to begin with but was even more chichi now that Jamie had arrived. Heads turned; Jamie was more than police. She practically made the day of the headwaiter.

As we sat down we both noticed a woman with cropped hair sitting across from us. She was maybe thirty-five, one of those no-makeup, intelligent, good-bones beauties. Jamie and I were both staring at her.

"I look at a woman like that in her understated gray sweater and perfect bones, and I want to cut all my hair off," Jamie confides to me. "Then I move right into 'I'm not beautiful enough.' I want to tell Versace to make me over, or, even better, I want to hide at the Gap forever."

I begin laughing. "I look at a woman like that, and I'm jealous that she can eat lamb chops."

Jamie and I both ordered a vegetable plate. As in every good

English restaurant, the vegetables are doused in butter. Jamie wiped hers off. I, of course, savored every encrusted morsel. I figured it had to have fewer calories than lamb chops.

As the meal progressed we reminisced about *The Heidi Chronicles* and began talking like girlfriends—well, new girl-friends. I told her about my mother, Lola, the dancer, and said that my father is very kind.

"Is your father kind?" I asked. We were friends reminiscing about childhood. I had completely forgotten that her father, along with being nice or not, was the star of *Operation Petticoat*.

After lunch we cruised the shops on Sloane Street. In the Nicole Farhi boutique we went through the sale racks and came across a few promising items.

"I hate dressing rooms and trying things on," Jamie told me as she slipped a skirt over her jeans in the middle of the shop. The salesladies were beside themselves. Jamie's attitude toward clothing is half negligent tomboy and half drop-dead glam-orous woman. It's very sexy and very honest.

When I dropped her at her Knightsbridge sublet, she asked me to come in and look at photos she had taken of her daugh-ter, Annie. Jamie Lee is a spectacular photographer.

Finally, however, she pulled out a picture she had not taken. It was an end-of-the-year photograph of a very English school. There were at least four hundred children in the photo, and Jamie asked me if I could find her daughter. I tried, but I couldn't distinguish her in the sea of faces.

"There she is. There's my girl," Jamie beamed. "I'm taking next year off to be with her. I know that a lot of women will think that's crazy. Maybe even she'll think it's crazy. But I want to do this for her. I want to do this for me."

The last time I saw Jamie she was being beamed by satellite into a convention of TV critics in Pasadena, California. I was sitting on the stage with our director and the producer. Jamie Lee was on a ladder on the balcony of a Paris hotel with the Arc de Triomphe behind her.

"So, Jamie Lee," the questioning began, "what do you think of Bob Dole's statement that *True Lies* is family entertainment?"

"I'm very happy with that movie and my role in it," she said, smiling and looking far more beautiful than any woman with cropped hair on the fifth floor of "Harvey Nick's." "And I think he's insane." The whole room of assembled critics burst into laughter.

"Jamie Lee, what's it like to have the best body in the business?" another hand in the Pasadena room shot up.

(I was reminded of a story Jamie Lee had told me about a photo shoot for the cover of *TV Guide* for *The Heidi Chronicles*. When Jamie Lee arrived at the photographer's studio, a twenty-one-year-old stylist had set out Thierry Mugler corsets and skintight minis, and Jamie refused to put on any of it. "This is a play about respect for women. I will not have it treated disrespectfully," Jamie had told her.)

Jamie shrugged off the body question, and the interrogation came back to me.

"Miss Wasserstein, what do you think of Jamie Lee's performance in *The Heidi Chronicles*?"

I looked up at her glowing in Paris. She couldn't even see me. "I think she's terrific. I think she's a wonderful serious actress."

Jamie Lee smiled. "I think all the women who have played Heidi on stage before me—Joan Allen, Brooke Adams, Christine Lahti, Mary McDonnell, and Amy Irving—were circling our set in a helicopter watching me. That's quite a legacy. They are all incredible actresses. But, of course," she went on to say, "people who were actually passing by and heard the title asked if I was making the Heidi Fleiss story."

"Is that true, Miss Wasserstein?" I was asked.

"Yes." I shook my head. "The extras asked me if Jamie was starring as Heidi Fleiss, the Beverly Hills Madam."

Jamie laughed. For a woman with the best body in the business, she also has the best take on herself of anybody in the business. Except she really doesn't know how really good she is.

Jill's Adventures in Real Estate;
or, I Can Get It for You at 3.2

VARSITY APARTMENTS, Eighty-fourth Street and First Avenue. The living room is squarish, the furniture is chromish, and the bookshelves IKEA-ish. Granita, twenty-eight, in Lycra, is Rollerblading; Christopher Wren IV, twenty-nine, in shades of paler blues, is reading Billy Baldwin Decorates; *and a couple are having sex as they watch* The Frugal Gourmet. *Jill Jeremy, twenty-eight, attractive, in jeans and Haverford sweatshirt, is reading the real estate section of the Sunday paper. She dials the phone.*

JILL (*on the phone*): Hello, is this Phyllis B. Phyllis, at Action Views? My name is Jill Jeremy, and I just saw your ad for a Chelsea studio, wood-burning fireplace, loads of light plus views, for six hundred and fifty dollars a month. I'm currently paying a thousand a month for a share, but I definitely want to keep the next rent in the three figures. I'm leaving my job to become a full-time short story writer. Something with character would be perfect. Monday at five-thirty would be great.

CHRISTOPHER: Jill, could you keep it down? I'm trying to read.

JILL: I'd also like a little privacy.

SCENE I

Chelsea studio, overlooking a brick wall. Phyllis B. Phyllis, in black dress, redder-than-red nails, and spike heels, is pulling contact paper off a minibar-sized refrigerator in the front closet.

PHYLLIS: The thing that is so fabulous about this apartment is that the kitchen is in the closet, which gives you so much more space.

JILL: Yes, that's convenient.

PHYLLIS: And I adore a brick view! It's so quiet! And I know you want to write.

JILL: I thought there was a fireplace.

PHYLLIS: Darling, there's plenty of room for a fireplace in any of these four walls. All this needs is a few window treatments and some color. And I've seen it look terrific without any furniture. Who's doing your apartment?

JILL: Doing?

PHYLLIS: Who's helping you?

JILL: I have a roommate who went to the Rhode Island School of Design. We can come back tomorrow.

PHYLLIS: But you really have to decide today if you want this. I have two other parties ready to make an offer. This is going to get snapped up. I think it's a little gem.

JILL: I really was hoping for something with a bit more charm.

PHYLLIS: For charm, you're going to have to go back up to four figures. I do have something on Bank Street that would be perfect for you. It's a sublet, fabulous light, and a very literary location. You've got Willa Cather, Charles Kuralt, Herbert Bergdorf, and Uta Hagen.

JILL: Who's that?

PHYLLIS: The famous actress from the original ice-cream family. Like I said, it's the ideal Old New York literary location. You'll think you're Edith Wharton. Trust me. This place isn't for you. This is junk. I know what you want.

SCENE 2

Bank Street. One-bedroom. A narrow, exposed-brick living room. All the other walls are painted black. Christopher Wren IV, wearing wire-rimmed glasses, inspects with Jill and Phyllis.

PHYLLIS: I'm so glad you're here, Christopher. I love people who know what they want. I just sold Brad Pitt a $2.6 million pied-à-terre, and it was the first apartment he saw. He walked in and knew right away. But, of course, Brad has such fabulous taste! I have to tell you that I love this apartment. Don't you think you can do something very cozy with this for Jill?

CHRISTOPHER: I'm feeling a little Holiday Inn, a little hanging ferns, a little S&M, and a little seriously seventies. What about the apartments across the street?

PHYLLIS: Well, those are the apartments across the street! Those are American classics! I just sold a house across the street to Linda Evangelista.

CHRISTOPHER: How much would Jill have to go up to get an apartment across the street?

PHYLLIS: I tell all my clients that once we're in the four-thousand-a-month bracket, which is what a nice apartment across the street would cost you, we really should start talking about buying, because the tax advantages make a lot more sense. That's what I told Sylvester Stallone's ex-girlfriend, and I found her the most fabulous loft in NoLisp.

JILL: Where's that?

PHYLLIS: North of Lispenard Street. Fabulous restaurants. Fabulous health clubs. And all the supermodels love it. You can even have breakfast with Harvey Keitel every morning.

SCENE 3

Law office of F. Bernard Aranoff, senior partner, tax division.

BERNARD: Find anything?

JILL: Phyllis B. Phyllis, at Action Views, tells me it makes more sense to buy a co-op.

BERNARD: Jill, you're a tax attorney and you're buying your first adult home. You don't use a nobody you found in the newspaper. I'm calling my agent right now. His name is Thomas Lee Edward, from the Edward Lee Edwards Agency. He's Henry Kissinger's real estate agent, but he's very sympathetic to artists. He found Robert Fulghum his apartment. You know, I am thrilled with Carnegie Hill. You really should consider it. It's a great family neighborhood, and you're within walking distance of all the best schools.

JILL: But I don't have any children.

BERNARD: Don't be so negative, Jill. You will someday. All our women associates have integrated lives.

JILL: Yes. Then you put them on the mommy track, so they don't make partner.

BERNARD: Beg your pardon?

JILL: I'd be happy to meet Thomas Lee Edward.

SCENE 4

Carnegie Hill. Very pastel-yellow children's bedroom overlooking a courtyard. Thomas Lee Edward, an affable young man in a blue suit, walks to the window and pulls open the duck-stenciled drapes. Christopher, Bernard, and Jill follow.

THOMAS: This is a great neighborhood for kids. It's near all the schools. And I think this is a great apartment. Louis Auchincloss once had lunch in this apartment.

BERNARD: Hear that, Jill? Jill's our firm's literary lion.

THOMAS: This happens to be a very artsy building. Your next-door neighbor arranges parties for Calvin Klein, and upstairs you've got C. Z. Guest's editor.

CHRISTOPHER: How much more would it be for something with a view of the park?

THOMAS: Then you're really getting into the million-dollar range. But if you can see your way to it, it's worth it. Especially for the resale value. I was having the same conversation with Tony Kushner just last week.

CHRISTOPHER: I think *Perestroika* is the greatest play of the twentieth century.

JILL (*talking rapidly*): How much did Tony Kushner make from that play? How much did Louis Auchincloss make from *The Rector of Justin?* What about John Grisham? Where does Scott Turow live? If I write *The Pelican Brief, Perestroika,* and *Presumed Innocent* next year, can I afford a view?

THOMAS: Tree level. On the second floor. Some people love it. Mark Hampton swears by the second floor.

JILL: What if I write *The Pelican Brief, Perestroika,* and *Presumed Innocent,* and I base a hit TV comedy series on all the junior tax associates, like *Friends* meets *Melrose Place,* only it's on Wall Street? I can call it *Happy Returns.*

THOMAS: Then you could be in the back on a higher floor. I love the back. Jed Johnson swears by the back. (*A nude man from the apartment across the courtyard begins waving at them.*) Some people like exhibitionists. Some people can't bear them. It's all a matter of taste. Parish-Hadley swears by exhibitionists.

SCENE 5

The Six Guys Coffee Shoppe. Jill and Granita, still in Lycra, having lunch.

GRANITA: So I said to him, I said, "Buzzy, you've got fear of commitment, and that's your problem, because I'm not just going to sit here and let my life go by while you work out your ambivalence." I said, "Buzzy, I'm twenty-six, I've got a great body, a brilliant career, and a hell of a lot of options." And you know what happened next?

JILL: He said, "You're not twenty-six, you're twenty-eight, and I'm leaving you for Alicia Silverstone."

GRANITA: He pulled out a fifty-thousand-dollar Bulgari engagement ring and said, "Marry me, Granita." Buzzy says we'll have a much bigger wedding than Marie-Chantal Miller and the Prince of Greece did, and bigger than any of her sisters' weddings, and I feel totally OK about that, because he's giving a matching grant for the entire cost to my favorite charity. And here's the best part, Robert Isabell is doing the flowers! So my life has worked out perfectly. And how are you?

JILL: I'm still looking for an apartment.

GRANITA: You know how I got Buzzy to marry me? I had to rope him in, wrestle him to the ground, and brand him. That's what you have to do with an apartment. Jill, you'll pardon my saying this, but you're being entirely too passive. You have to use my agent Rosalee Rose, at Wells, Wells & Wells. She's already found for me the most wonderful little Stanford White house, on Gramercy Park. It used to be the Players Club.

JILL: I don't want a house. I want a studio apartment.

GRANITA: Sh-h-h! And you have to get rid of Christopher Wren and use my decorator, Bario Baronial.

JILL: Who?

GRANITA: What do you mean, who? Everyone knows Bario. He's the Baron of Baronial. Bario has single-handedly brought back the Robber Baron style. Don't you ever read *House & Homes?* He's practically on the cover every issue. Are you listening to me?

JILL: I was thinking maybe I should change my name to an ice.

SCENE 6

Park Avenue living room, an enormous room with fireplace and molding. Bario Baronial, around forty with handlebar mustache and wearing a suit similar to one of Cornelius Vanderbilt's; Rosalee Rose

in a tasteful business suit and Hermès scarf; Granita in Versace
Lycra; and Jill.

GRANITA: It's really just a maid's room. And it's too much
light.

BARIO: Well, you could darken it down with wood pan-
eling, large leather wing chairs, heavy chandeliers, velvet
drapes, and rhino horns.

ROSALEE: You could also knock down the walls to the dining room and the study.

BARIO: The thing about these Park Avenue apartments is
they're all really too small. I just had the same conversation
with Barbara Walters. That's why the Carnegies, the Vander-
bilts, and the Warburgs all built houses. The problem is
they're all museums now, and it's very hard to get Landmarks
Preservation to permit you to turn a museum into a private
home.

ROSALEE: But it can be done. I just sold David Geffen the
Metropolitan Museum and all its contents.

GRANITA: The Met would really be too big for Jill. But is
the Cooper-Hewitt for sale?

BARIO: How about the Frick? I love that cloister.

GRANITA: I'll look into it.

ROSALEE: Have you considered Central Park West?

GRANITA: I hate the West Side.

ROSALEE: What do you think, Jill?

JILL: I don't know who I am anymore. Some days I'm Carnegie Hill Jill and other days I'm NoLisp Jill. How can I be the same person and a hundred blocks apart?

ROSALEE: But if you want to write and you're not moving to the Hamptons or Jackson Hole, the West Side is really the place to be. By the way, our office does handle Jackson Hole. I've sold a lot of ranches to former New Yorkers. Have you considered a ranch, Jill?

BARIO: Speaking of ranches, what about the Dakota?

ROSALEE: I've got a co-broke in the Dakota.

SCENE 7

The Dakota, Central Park West. First floor. The original furnace room. A homeless man is sleeping on a bench in front of the window. Rosalee, in a new, crisp suit, enters with Jill. Phyllis has opened the door. She wears her signature spikes.

ROSALEE: Hello, Phyllis. I'd like you to meet Jill Jeremy.

PHYLLIS: I know Jill. Every real estate agent in New York knows Jill. Do you know what we call you? Jill, the Show-Me State. I thought we had an exclusive, Jill.

JILL: But I never—

PHYLLIS: You're dishonorable, Jill.

JILL: But I never—

ROSALEE: Is this true?

JILL: Yes. I saw apartments with Phyllis.

ROSALEE: Who else have you been seeing apartments with, Jill? We'll find out. We all know each other.

JILL: Thomas Lee Edward at Edward Lee Edwards, Robbie Robb at L. Douglas Mann, John Bedsheets at Brownie, Harry & Stevie, Big Mac Parks at Scribbling & More Scribbling.

ROSALEE: Jill, you've seen over two hundred apartments. Have you talked to a psychiatrist about this? You're getting a very bad reputation. You need to work on your decision making.

JILL: I really, really like this apartment. I really, really want to live here. I'm really, really happy you're co-brokering so you can split the commission. How much is this apartment?

PHYLLIS and ROSALEE: Three point five million. But the owner is negotiable at three point two.

ROSALEE: I think you'll be very happy here. It's a great buy. I've got six other people coming back this afternoon.

PHYLLIS: You've looked for so long—just make a bid.

ROSALEE: I wouldn't let you take any place if you wouldn't

be happy with it. And I can always turn this around and sell it. It's a great professional space.

JILL: What about the man sleeping in front of my window?

ROSALEE: Have you read the Alan Bennett diaries? Did you read about the lady who lived on his lawn? The book was a best-seller in England. You can write about the man who sleeps in your window.

SCENE 8

Law office of F. Bernard Aranoff, senior partner, tax division.

JILL: They accepted my offer. What should I do?

BERNARD: Do you love the apartment?

JILL: I need someplace to live.

BERNARD: Three point five million is a lot of money to pay because you need somewhere to live.

JILL: There was a bidding war.

BERNARD: Look, Jill, now that you've decided to work double time and sell your parents' house and their car and your law degree and your grandmother's entire rare Stickley Arts and Crafts furniture collection plus write five television series and ghostwrite Newt's next five novels in order to afford an apartment, get something that you love.

JILL: But Rosalee and Phyllis will be furious.

BERNARD: They're real estate agents. We'll call Thomas Lee Edward.

JILL: He's furious, too.

BERNARD: He's a real estate agent. Besides, he just sold the Empire State Building to Sir Andrew Lloyd Webber. He wanted a loft with great views, high ceilings, and a rehearsal studio. But I understand there are a few studios left in the tower.

SCENE 9

Empire State Building. Tower. A studio apartment. The room is squarish, the furniture is chromish, and the bookshelves IKEA-ish. The view is magnificent. There are paper plates everywhere. Granita, Bario, Christopher, Bernard, and Jill follow Thomas to the window.

THOMAS: Sir Andrew had a party here last night.

GRANITA: It's so charming that he uses paper plates. I get a very good feel from that.

THOMAS: I happen to know that Martha Stewart was here last night and she says that this apartment has the best bathroom in New York. And I know that Steven Spielberg looked at this apartment and loved it, but Kate insisted they needed more than a studio. He was also at the party last night.

BERNARD: Who else was here?

THOMAS: Johnny Depp, Jayne Anne Phillips, President Chirac, Elizabeth Hurley, Anna Sui, Ronald Perelman, Forrest Sawyer, Ice T, Mark Morris, Colin Powell, Howell Raines, Christopher Darden, Nicholas Hytner, Naomi Campbell, James Lovell, Miss Divine Brown, Senator Alan Simpson, David Bouley, Donna Hanover Giuliani, and Betty Buckley.

BERNARD: I think you should take it.

CHRISTOPHER: You won't even have to light it at night. It'll automatically be orange for Halloween, and red-white-and-blue for the Fourth of July.

BARIO: Take it.

GRANITA: Take it.

BERNARD: Take it.

CHRISTOPHER: Take it.

THOMAS: Take it.

JILL: All right. I'll take it. How much?

THOMAS: Seven million. But I think we can get it for six point five. (*The song "Memory" begins flooding through the window.*) I forgot to tell you. As a gift to the city of New York, Sir Andrew has arranged for cats to dance up and down the spire every hour. And it's included in the maintenance.

EPILOGUE

The Charlie Rose *show. A studio on Park Avenue. A round table and chair. Charlie and Jill sit across from each other.*

CHARLIE: I understand you wrote six best-sellers this year in order to afford an apartment and you're still a tax attorney.

JILL: Yes, Charlie.

CHARLIE: Have you found an apartment yet?

JILL: No. And I've seen over two thousand of them.

CHARLIE: I have to move on Friday and I've got nowhere to go. My landlord sold my house. Do you have the name of a real estate agent?

JILL: Charlie, I've *become* a real estate agent, because they all stopped talking to me, and Thomas Lee Edward retired because of me and moved to New Zealand. I just sold Michael Eisner the Metropolitan Opera House for *Disney/ABC News on Ice.* I'd be happy to take you out looking.

CHARLIE: Can I ask where you are living now?

JILL: The Y, on Ninety-second and Lexington. It costs me six hundred and fifty dollars a month.

CHARLIE: Jill Jeremy, best-selling author, tax attorney, and real estate agent, thanks for joining me. Good night.

JILL: Thank you, Charlie. Good night.

Women Beware Women

Women are the worst. I will rot in hell for saying that. My toes will gnarl inward into tiny hooves, and I'll never dare to get another pedicure. All right. All right. Women are kind, decent, nurturing, the best friends women could ever have—until they're not. Then women can be the absolute worst.

When I was growing up my least favorite movies were the ones that came on television at around three o'clock in the afternoon on Sundays in which Joan Crawford or Bette Davis in a skintight sequined suit and shoulder pads to the sky deliberately set out to steal her best friend's husband. The action seemed completely implausible to me. Of course, I was in the fifth grade at the time and was not about to run off with my best friend Susan's husband. But these lady schemers were clearly evil, manipulating Jezebels and clearly could only succeed on celluloid. In real life women friends were always good to each other forever and ever. Right?

Looking back, this childhood optimism was very nice and naive. At summer camp I was once the object of a "hate club." The girls in my bunk got together and decided to turn on me just for fun. We were around twelve at the time, and to this day I'm not sure if they objected to my unruly curly hair, to my odd interest in theater and history books, or simply to the fact that I wasn't as fascinated by the opposite sex as they were.

This is not to say that I am always the victim. I've learned. I have my mean streaks. I moved out on my college roommate at a time when she thought we were the closest of friends. She was too smart; I was flunking. I've been told secrets, sworn never to utter them to another living soul, and immediately picked up the phone to spill the beans. I've not returned phone calls, I've not precisely said what has been on my mind, and I've even decided to make new friends and lose touch with the old. Bottom line, as long as I'm confessing: I've even slept with a friend's former lover, and if she thought that was good sex, I'm glad I'm not plotting to sleep with her husband.

But I have never been mean. Really aggressively mean. I've always thought female friendships are at all costs to be protected. They should be sources of peace and security rather than anxiety and discomfort. A Tuesday night when you haven't heard from a man who should be calling is cause for a little heart flutter, but a Tuesday night when your best friend hasn't called in a week is time for panic.

Let's face it, though—some women betray other women. For them, other women are fine company until a man shows up. I know a woman who befriended a number of single gals when she got divorced. But as soon as she landed a mate she dropped the women like hot potatoes. From her point of view, these new single friends could only be jealous of her newfound fortune. Her new single friends could only be a threat.

Because our jealousies are limited mostly to our own gender, most women I know compete with each other and not with men. (A boyfriend of a very glamorous and dear friend of mine once told me that my friend hung out with far less glamorous-looking women in order to make herself look good.

In a huff I told him that I was one of those women she hung out with and that couldn't possibly be true.) A woman I know slept with her best friend's powerful father-in-law partially to prove that not only could she compete but she could win, hands down. Many women I know have gay male friends because you get the intimacy and conversation available from a sensitive female friend without the competition.

The basis of friendship should be trust. But with women the slightest infringement becomes betrayal. In a romantic relationship the breach can be solved with screaming arguments and even sex. With women friends it's much harder. A woman I know stopped talking to me because she felt I hadn't acknowledged her properly in a social situation. She was, in fact, right. It was a party in my honor, and I was distracted. I tried calling her on the phone, and she wouldn't answer. I tried writing letters stating my argument and received a postcard back with one line: "Thank you for your note." Being an obsessive masochist, I even sent her a rather grand fortieth-birthday gift. It was important to me to get this right.

My friend and I would run into each other from time to time, and we would always be cordial. But I was, frankly, brokenhearted. New friends never really know how sad you are when a parent is sick because they weren't there when you truly hated your mother. Finally, after years went by, we began to send each other notes marking life's happy and sad occasions. My friend and I now see each other for dinner occasionally. We'll never talk every day on the phone. We'll never be able to hurt each other in the way that we both did before. But I love her very much. And I feel calmer knowing that problem has finally been solved.

The closer the friendship, the more anguished the rupture. A woman I know fixed her best friend up with a man she was quite close to. They began dating, and moved in together, and cut the matchmaker completely out of their lives. It seems the friendship was a crutch the best friend didn't need anymore. I have also known women to panic at their best friends' success. Often it's not the success story who moves on but the envious companion. It is not unknown for a best friend not to show up at an opening night or a celebration dinner.

Perhaps the joy of women's friendships is also its undoing. Female friendship isn't just about shoe shopping and diets. Women friends know the entire story. They are sources of reason, great joy, and even femininity. There's no greater sense of complete security and toleration than with a woman friend. But there's no formal structure. Nowhere for it to go. Friends don't get married or even move in together. Since they generally, no matter how close, become secondary in each other's lives, friends—and friendships—move on.

I was recently at an all-women fiftieth-birthday party. The birthday girl was a beloved wife and friend and even has a good reputation in business. But what was most impressive at this brunch was she had known most of the women there for ten or twenty years. Three friends got up and read a limerick all about her past love life, work, and travails. And at the end they finished their poem with "We should know. We're your best friends." The signature of a truly enviable woman is the tenacity and continuity of her women friends.

Designing Men

ike Brady, the *Brady Bunch* dad, is a guy with princi-
ples and bell-bottom trousers. He's an architect who
built his own kind of house, and he has his own kind
of retro family values. If he were a crooner, he'd be belting
nightly an Our Gang version of "My Way" at the Sears, Roe-
buck bar-and-grill. Mike Brady, much like Gary Cooper as the
classic cinema architect Howard Roark in *The Fountainhead,* is
willing to stand up for his beliefs and manly enough to follow
through.

But Mike is a sensitive guy, too. He reads *Jonathan Liv-
ingston Seagull* in bed, and is a caring husband and loving dad.
He even has artistic integrity. In *The Brady Bunch Movie* his
designs consistently bear more than a passing resemblance to
77 *Sunset Strip,* but he doesn't budge from his vision. Mike's
split-level gas station is his Robie House.

Of course, Mike isn't the only sensitive but wholly hetero
hero who has appeared on the silver screen lately. In fact, architects are the movie men of the moment—the perfect combo of
the old male and the new. Movie architects wear T-shirts and
jeans and have unstructured, Dolce & Gabbana or Banana
Republic silhouettes, but they are quite capable of holding

their own with prominent men in business suits. They're artists who have no problem with numbers. Developers are evil movie bad guys, willing to throw over the environment just for a condo. But architects, though initially cool and withholding, are on the side of good.

Movie architects tend to be hunky and tall, like Gary Cooper, and unlike the real-life shortish greats—Frank Lloyd Wright, Louis I. Kahn, and I. M. Pei. Among the recent crop on screen were the sweet and widowed Tom Hanks, in *Sleepless in Seattle;* the befuddled but secretly sweet Woody Harrelson, in *Indecent Proposal;* and Jeff Bridges, the Good Samaritan plane-crash survivor, in *Fearless.* When Bridges lets the husband of a distressed fellow survivor know that he's an architect, the husband is reassured of his seriousness.

It takes a real man to romance a Romanesque curve. Richard Gere, in *Intersection,* plays an architect trapped at a midlife crossroads between Sharon Stone, his coolly elegant wife, and Lolita Davidovich, his wilder, younger journalist lover. Tom Selleck, in *Three Men and a Baby,* is an architect so secure in his masculinity that he bonds adorably with his baby girl by bringing her to a building site in a small pink hard hat. It's a detail she might well mention to her therapist—along with the three men—in the future.

Until recently, film architects, like cowboys, had no ethnic affiliation. Sam Waterston, in *Hannah and Her Sisters,* is from the innovative and socially agile school of Robert A. M. Stern, Hugh Hardy, and Charles Gwathmey—the ultimate gentleman architect, well versed in opera and the Flatiron District. In more recent films, the education and vita are the same but the background is more diverse: Wesley Snipes, for example, plays an architect trapped by his classical and classist taste in Spike Lee's interracial romance, *Jungle Fever.* The current champion of architect casting, David Strathairn, plays the over-

worked—and possibly Jewish or at least not totally Waspy—
architect husband of Jessica Lange in *Losing Isaiah* and of
Meryl Streep in *The River Wild*. (Obviously, architects prefer
blondes.)

Of course, there are other sensitive but masculine film voca-
tions: James Woods is a veterinarian in *Immediate Family,* and
Burt Reynolds is a sculptor in *The Man Who Loved Women*. But
to someone scanning the possibilities for attractive new-male
careers, a book editor seems too intellectual, a film director too
autocratic, a doctor too open to malpractice, an investment
banker too "eighties," a talent agent too scuzzy, a personal
trainer too Fabio, a lawyer too insistent on an unromantic
prenup, a congressman too Republican to pair with the likes
of Jessica or Meryl, and a college professor too low-salaried,
too politically correct, and maybe even too potentially gay.

"A building has integrity, just like a man," Howard Roark
asserts to his critics. Film architects have the instincts of
artists and the responsibilities of real men. They are never elitist, because, bottom line, they care about how we live—about
the nitty-gritty, the bathrooms, the kitchen sinks. Most important, metaphorically and concretely, an architect can always "get it up."

The Muse That Mewed

I don't come from a long line of pet lovers. One of my earliest memories is of my mother, Lola, releasing our pet parakeet into a hurricane. She never explained how the bird flew out of her cage into the storm, but all we children knew it was involuntary. And then there was the time I came home from elementary school to find our newly acquired cocker spaniel on the roof. My mother swore that the dog had climbed up there for the view, but I certainly had never seen Lassie on the roof. The police arrived, and the dog survived and subsequently moved to live with relatives in the suburbs. The last straw was my father driving a cat from our house in Brooklyn over the bridge into Manhattan and dropping her off somewhere near Wall Street, apparently hoping that a generous stockbroker would take her in or perhaps she would become a cub of the Dreyfus lion. Personally, I thought my entire family should have been brought in for questioning by the animal-rights board.

Ten years ago I advised a single friend of mine who was thinking about getting a dog that we had to try people first and then move on to animals. Within six months I had a cat, Ginger, and he a dog, Phyllis.

Ginger the cat had at least one life before she met me. I found her as an adult at the ASPCA and have no idea where she lived before. Ginger and I did not have love at first sight. In fact, it was my friend André who first spotted her. Actually it was André who dragged me to the ASPCA to begin with. He was a cat lover, the owner of the late, great Pussers, a gray aristocrat with elegant lines, and he persuaded me to drop my fears of becoming a LSWWC—Lonely Single Woman with Cats—and replace them with the joy of having a warm, intelligent feline by the fire.

Ginger was never a calendar cat. We chose her because she was an orange calico, and if I had to have a cat I didn't want a czarina like Pussers but rather a fuzzy orange Creamsicle. My veterinarian, Dr. Ann Lucas, says Ginger was between three and four years old when we first met her and always had an older cat's teeth and personality. That was fine—frankly, I didn't want a Puffy jumping around the house with a ball of yarn. I had read once in an Ann Beattie interview about her cats sitting on the windowsill as the light flooded in on a bright winter day when the delicate and talented writer sat down to work. I wanted old Ginger with her dark sad eyes seated beside me like a sheepdog as the evening light faded on my day's literary travels.

You can't always get what you want. Forget Puffy— Ginger's voice and personality verged on Linda Blair's in *The Exorcist*. Unlike the millionaire singing kitty who croons about her love for chicken and liver, Ginger had a grating, prolonged meow that sounded like Ethel Merman holding a note after belting "I can do anything better than you." At any moment I thought her head would swivel and she would inform me that my mother sucked bad things that rhymed with clocks in hell. Every morning at five o'clock she would tap my head and hair until I served up her favorite turkey Fancy Feast. On four cans of Fancy Feast a day, sad-eyed Ginger and a furry Dallas Cowboys football soon became indistinguishable.

During my life with Ginger our personalities began to merge: Ginger preferred resting by the radiator to any physical activity, and so did I. When a new married man arrived in our home, Ginger perked herself up, became immediately charming and attentive, and lost all interest in me. I too have been known to become obsessed by a gentleman caller and cancel a date with an understanding friend. Ginger believed all things could be solved by a snack and a phone call, and so did I. After a day's activities, I would call my neighbor Michi to chat, and Ginger would jump on the bed and pull on the phone cord. Finally, I began leaving messages for Aunt Michi from Ginger ranging from her thoughts on Socks the White House cat to her feline opinions of me. Ginger thought I should stay home all day just like her. I would certainly get more work done and wouldn't get involved with narcissists who reminded her of Felix the Cat.

During my life with Ginger I wrote better and more happily than ever before. While I was at the desk, she didn't sit on the windowsill but on the bed. I would finish a scene, get on the bed to rest, and we would look it over together. I was thirty-six years old, writing my play *The Heidi Chronicles,* and she was probably 102, but I always thought of us as a girl and her cat. And at the end of a particularly satisfying Saturday evening at home in a Lanz flannel nightgown, I would watch Ginger's TV idol Toonces the driving cat on *Saturday Night Live.* Toonces was the feline version of George Maharis in *Route 66.* This kitty—not a computer actualization but a kitty as real as Ginger—got behind the wheel of his convertible weekly and took to the road. Ginger, who had never been impressed by her mention in *The Heidi Chronicles* (as the famous children's book *King Ginger the Lion*), sat on my lap for *Saturday Night Live* because our neighbor, her Aunt Michi, knew someone at the show and therefore could introduce her to Toonces.

Toonces died of cancer at age nine. Ginger died of bladder cancer at age twelve or maybe, according to Dr. Lucas, at fourteen. All I know is that both passed away last year. I found out about her diagnosis while I was working on a play in London. As I look back on it, I was told I would have to fly to New York and close *The Sisters Rosensweig* and my cat on the same weekend. I know plays have to close, but I had no idea I would be losing my companion, my best source of funny anecdotes, my friend through mostly thick and seldom thin. When Ginger had first arrived at my home, I wrote a song medley for her of Ginger's greatest hits—including "Rootilda," sung to "Matilda" using her nickname "Root," as in *gingerroot*. I had no idea that the pleasure of Ginger sitting on my stomach over the Sunday *Times* and our singing a duet of "Rootilda"—her Linda Blair falsetto and my Harry Belafonte—would become a memory. I was very jealous this past Christmas when I saw the MTV video of those caroling kitties. If only Ginger had survived two more months, I could have been a stage mother.

Ginger was diagnosed for her final curtain in early July. She survived until November. Ginger, who developed a taste for not only Fancy Feast but the dramatic during her stay with me, had an *On Golden Pond* finale: I believe in the last months of her life Ginger fell in love.

A doctor I respect once told me that treating cancer is like chasing a fish: you watch where it swims and take it from there. Ginger certainly wasn't swimming upstream, but she wasn't drowning either. While I had to be in London I hired a handsome young man named Ken to move in with Ginger. Suddenly Ginger made a miraculous (albeit short-term) recovery—kidney counts were down and Kenny Cassillo was in the air. She followed him around the house and stared at him lovingly while he sat at the desk. At last I had a son-in-law. Every week that last summer, Cindy, my assistant, and beloved Kenny packed up Ginger and took her in a Town Car to Dr. Lucas. Ginger always traveled first-class. She was Orphan Annie—the cat who made it from the ASPCA to Fifth Avenue. No public transportation for her. At the end of her life she even switched from Fancy Feast to Hadleigh's Gourmet Shoppe sliced turkey.

During the fall, when I was living at home again, she became incontinent, but as long as her blood levels were acceptable and she wasn't in pain, I was still chasing that fish. Finally, in November while I was in Los Angeles for a week, Cindy called me to say she thought it was time.

Ken and I took Ginger down to Dr. Lucas for her final visit. She sat in my lap, now very thin and very sweet, and I lifted her to the window. "Look at the world, Ginger," I told her. I wanted her to know where she was leaving so she could tell stories where she was going.

I couldn't bear to go home that afternoon. I got back on a plane to Los Angeles, and as I looked out the window at a flash of orange in the sky I thought of the Elton John song about Daniel waving goodbye. But Ginger wasn't saying goodbye; she was on her way to meet Toonces in his red convertible and drive to visit our friend Harry Kondoleon, the playwright who had been chasing an immune-deficient fish for the past five years.

I imagined Harry greeting Ginger: "It's you. Come in. I have cans and cans of Fancy Feast. How is Wendy? Everyone up here knows you wrote all her plays."

And sometimes I think she did.

Heidi Chronicled

During my years in the mid-sixties at the Calhoun School in New York, the greatest hits of female preparatory-school drama departments were largely of the convent and weeping-widow genre: *Cradle Song* and García Lorca's *The House of Bernarda Alba*. Also popular were the abbreviated *Trojan Women* and the mini *Lysistrata*. At Calhoun, during the *gaudeamus igitur* curtain call of the annual Latin-class Saturnalia show, the Velcro hooks on our Fieldcrest twin-sheet togas came unfastened, proving for all the parent body the true value of a classical education: *Nulla res melior spectaculo est*—or, very roughly, there's no business like show business.

In the late 1960s, when junior-year women were admitted to the male bastions of ivy, the walls of single-sex education came tumbling down. Amherst College, for instance, experimented with the very balanced ratio of 23 in-house females, of which I made up a twenty-third, to 1,200 males. Rather than in convent plays, I was suddenly appearing nightly in leather as Beryl the Dominatrix in a dormitory-basement production of Terrence McNally's one-act, *Noon*. For my senior year, I returned to Mount Holyoke and the comfort of an all-female audience.

Twenty-five years later, and a month after Jamie Lee Curtis wrapped her film portrayal as Heidi Holland in my play *The Heidi Chronicles*, Anna Cash made her ninth-grade debut in the Brearley School all-female production. The entire upper school was present for the performance. Sitting in the balcony were the proud parents, mostly in their forties and looking suspiciously like academics, doctors, and assorted serious good people. Indeed, Anna Cash's mother is the novelist Mary Gordon.

If "The Rime of the Ancient Mariner" is about a man who shot a bird, *The Heidi Chronicles* is about a feminist art historian who gets sad. The play follows the life of Heidi—not the goat girl or the Beverly Hills matchmaker—from a Miss Crain's school dance in 1965 to her choice to adopt a baby alone in 1989. In the Brearley interpretation, Anna Cash appeared and began the play's opening monologue—an art history lecture about ignored women artists—in front of a slide painting by Sofonisba Anguissola (circa 1559). The upper school at Brearley is apparently big on irony: Miss Cash got a house laugh on "This portrait can be perceived as a meditation on the brevity of youth, beauty, and light—but what can't?" On Broadway, the line often didn't even get an educated smirk.

The girls giggled through the Miss Crain's dance scene. Tenley Laserson was very hip as Chip Boxer, the cool boy in Weejuns and a tweed jacket, still a familiar type at first-rate female prep schools. When Rachel Grand as Scoop Rosenbaum asked Heidi to go to bed with him in the 1968 Eugene McCarthy mixer scene, I noted the first bit of revisionism. In *The Heidi Chronicles* for grown-ups, Scoop says he can't promise Heidi "equal orgasms." At Brearley, Scoop couldn't promise Heidi an "equal relationship." The most interesting bit of nineties invention came in the women's-rap-group scene.

Fran, a physicist, was described in an Ann Arbor women's-consciousness-raising rap group in 1970 as an "open" lesbian. In my original text, she is merely a lesbian. Clearly, the Brearley ninth grade has had discussions on open and closed sexual preference. Anna Cash, like Jamie Lee Curtis, ended the rap-group scene singing and dancing Aretha Franklin's "Respect" as the women celebrated feminism and all that it promised for their future. When, after the performance, I asked the cast if the play seemed pertinent to them, Rebecca Mancuso, who played Fran, smiled through her braces. "The women's-movement stuff was the most fun," she said. "We all loved that."

I remember returning to Mount Holyoke on Sunday nights in the late sixties after a weekend in New Haven or Hanover. (You never revealed the name of the college you were dating if you had any savvy.) Finally, the stress of a weekend away pretending not to be who we really were was over, and we'd sit for hours in flannel shirts and jeans, smart women just talking. As I left the Brearley School a few weeks ago, I passed through the lunchroom, and there was a new generation of smart women talking about life, men, Heidegger, and *The Heidi Chronicles*. *Nulla res melior feminae re*—or, very roughly, there's no business like women's business.

The Me I'd Like to Be

Open wide on the city, maybe a little Gershwin playing, or Tony Bennett crooning a low "Since I Fell for You." Then a long slow climb up a long slow leg, a leg that lasts forever. Suddenly there's a conversation going on between a man and a woman. He's nuts about her. She's so secure, she blows him away. It's the kind of self-assurance that makes everyone around her think, I must be OK because she's OK.

She tells him that in the past six weeks she has decided to love her work, make peace with her mother, turn every possible emotional outburst into verse poetry, and learn his favorite sport, hang gliding. Moreover, she now looks at all the younger women whom he constantly ogles as valuable colleagues and friends. The camera zooms in close, very close, on the man as his eyes bulge out of their sockets like two Slinkys in heat. "Boy, babe," he says, now gasping for breath. "You sure have changed. Yes sir. I think I'm really gonna like the brand-new you."

The clock strikes 2:45 a.m. Sinatra's singing, "Make it one for my baby and one more for the road." Magic time is over. She pulls off the mask, unfastens that long, long prosthetic leg, and begins complaining about her work, her mother, and his wandering eye and bursts into uncontrollable-yet-familiar sobs. "I shoulda known better. You'll

131

never change," he grunts as he leaves with the fourteen-year-old Gap
model from across the room.

Close on the woman as she slams her face into a cold bacon-
cheeseburger. "As God is my witness," she says, picking up the ice-cold,
ketchup-sopping bun, "next year I will be different."

Radical change, the kind that gives you a shot at a second or
third chance, has always been my favorite fantasy. Not quite
as radical a change as, say, Christine Jorgensen or Renee
Richard—gender bending might be too ambitious—but I've
always craved someone noticing a turn for the better.

Perhaps what is required is something on the order of a
high school report card: "Wendy has really grown this year in
French. Her vocabulary has improved, and she has demonstrated remarkable new maturity and avid class participation."
Moreover, and this is the post–high school addendum, "She
approaches her life calmly and discerningly. She continues to
be generous but never wimpy and has conquered her fatal
attraction to jacks, pick up sticks, and all other stationary
activities."

Frankly, physical changes are the easiest to get across.
Of course, no one in semipolite society says, "Gee, you look
terrific—you've had your eyes lifted, your neck removed, and
your lips jet-puffed," after extensive cosmetic surgery. But
they certainly do notice.

Far more difficult is letting people know you've tried to
make some internal changes like being slightly less defensive,
slightly more open, or even willing to reveal a hint of assertion
and newfound self-worth. No one meets an old friend for a
drink and says, "Gee, I'm amazed. You've developed a sense of
worth. Are you sure you're all right?"

It would be nice to think that personal growth is an end in

itself and it doesn't matter what people think. Except that changes like being less defensive or more open are useless unless there is someone to be more open or less defensive with.

One way to get noticed is to make the sweeping personal change: divorce twice in a year, move the entire family to the Republic of Georgia, or give up law and take a job demonstrating a step machine with Bruce Jenner on cable television at three o'clock in the morning. But there must be a middle ground like being willing to order meat at a table full of vegetarians or actually telling a friend you feel slightly different.

Every year I make a proposed list of improvements. Actually, twice a year I make a list—at New Year's and in September, the beginning of the school year. There are always practical changes brought forward on the list from the previous year, like commit to flossing in a big way.

But the more important ones are harder to define. Every year I resolve to believe there will be possibilities. Every year I resolve to be a little less like the me I know and leave a little room for the me I could be. Every year I make a note not to feel left behind by my friends and family who have managed to change far more than I.

Getting off a plane in Los Angeles the other week, I noticed a young woman in blue jeans checking out her belly button ring, and I decided perhaps the answer to this change dilemma is body piercing.

The camera pans on a couple, old friends maybe, having drinks at a local joint. He's an accountant; she's an attorney. Suddenly she lifts her shirt jacket to reveal a diamond stud in her belly button. Now he knows something's afoot. Now he knows she's moving on. He's about to

*say something, but instead he opens his Brooks Brothers shirt to reveal
a Cartier engagement ring right through his left pectoral.*

So I'm thinking maybe next year I won't make a list of all
these proposed changes I desperately need to make in order to
impressively get on with my life. Maybe I'll approach it all a
little calmly. Maybe I won't concentrate on the thinnest person who is at least ten years younger than I am in every movie
I see and decide by next year I must mutate into her or go into
complete seclusion. Maybe I will try to be less defensive about
insisting my friends notice how I've turned my life around.
Maybe I will just relax. That would be an enormous change.

Mom Says Every Day
Is Mother's Day

Every day is Mother's Day. Just ask my mother, Lola Wasserstein. However, should one decide to pay homage on the appointed time of recognition, Lola does offer a few key pointers. For instance, there's no need to give rubies or emeralds when something from the heart, a personal expression, would be so much more appreciated.

A mother prefers a homemade creation, a child's own handicraft, to any storebought jewel or bauble. My mosaic ashtrays, multicolored whistle lanyards, tile hot plates, and elastic-band potholders saved my father fortunes at Cartier and Tiffany.

For those children who are more verbally than visually creative, Lola encourages sending "the very, very best," a homemade greeting card. A personal citation like "I love you, Gramma" or "Mother, I promise next year to be married with three musically inclined children, a co-op, and a degree in dentistry" is worth thousands of words.

Actually, in the early days of my family, we officially celebrated Mother's Day. We ventured en masse in the mid-1950s to Lundy's Restaurant in Sheepshead Bay, Brooklyn, for seafood.

According to my mother, it was a beautiful occasion. My grandmother wore a corsage, and the children looked beautiful and were beautifully behaved.

I, on the other hand, recall a vast, dark, medieval hall where waiters shoved past balancing platters piled high with steamers and lobster tails, and my brother and I tossed hot biscuits.

And I do remember a few tranquil luncheons at the Russian Tea Room before I had any idea that a seat in a bar booth could lead to a movie contract and being internationally creatively managed by ICM, CAA, or William Morris.

Mostly, however, my family has adhered to the "Every day is Mother's Day" solution. The upside of this attitude results in there being no need for me to run to Saks to find my mother the perfect lingerie or handbag to give her tomorrow.

But this good-works approach to Mother's Day, while admirable, has also led in my lifetime to bringing home a 99 on a school test and my mother inquiring "Where's the other point?" If every day is Mother's Day, she merits a full 100 percent daily. Frankly, sometimes I would have rather gone to Saks for a nightgown.

A friend and I had an idea that Mother's Day could be transformed into a The Happiness My Children Have Brought Me competition. In Yiddish this would translate into "The Naches Invitational." It could be held yearly at Miami's Fontainebleau or the Arizona Biltmore, and each mother would have an opportunity to compete for titles like Most Supportive Mother, Most Demanding Mother, and Mother with the Family of Most Practicing Attorneys. But Lola pointed out that mothers are much more interested in seeing their children than competing with each other.

So once again I will be sure to visit. And I will tell her once again she mustn't call any more of my aunts to tell them my play won the Nobel Prize. Every day may be Mother's Day, but I'm not on my way to Stockholm.

She'll show me every card from her nine grandchildren and tell me how each of them could be a brilliant artist or writer, but she hopes they'll all marry and have families, too. By the end of the visit, I'll think it's definitely time to go home, and she'll ask one more leading question hoping to hear I've secretly been married these past ten years, or have arranged to spend the entire summer at a health spa.

But when we part, all the memories of mosaic ashtrays, the biscuits at Lundy's, and "Where's the other point?" will come flooding back. I'll wonder if I will ever be selfless enough to think of myself as a mother first, as my mother, Lola, does.

And just when I become most sentimental, full of love and deep respect, I'll tell her, "Happy Mother's Day, Lola." Then, as she does every year, she'll turn to me with a sly: "Don't call me Lola, and I don't celebrate Mother's Day. You know, every day is Mother's Day."

Waif Goodbye, Hello Bulge

The trend began inauspiciously. "Wanderful" was discovered eating biscuits and gravy at a Hardee's in Independence, Kansas. Looking back, we really can't say whether it was fate or natural selection that brought our fashion editor to the booth beside her. Our woman in Independence was scouring the heartland for the next waif, the next naturally 105-pound, five-foot-eight sixteen-year-old who eats like a horse, never exercises, and has a face that could launch a million underwear ads.

It wasn't that Wanderful was eating double portions of biscuits with gravy that mesmerized our editor; it was the fact that she *looked* like someone who ate double portions of biscuits. Wanderful's arms were three times the size of her wrists, as opposed to the popular waifs, whose wrists, arms, and thighs all have the same diameter. Our editor was riveted. She wondered if Wanderful had had lipo-insertion to get those arms.

When Wanderful got up from her booth, our editor noticed her fitted dress didn't quite close. Furthermore, along her back there was a rippling effect. As Wanderful paid the bill and loosened her belt, gasping with relief, fashion history was made. For our editor, everything suddenly clicked: Aerobicized, sculpted bodies were the look of the self-indulgent late eighties, and waifs were the image of the politically correct ascetic nineties, but for the twenty-first century hips would be pips, and Wanderful had them. It would be the millennium of womanliness.

When our editor approached Wanderful and asked her name, weight, and height, Wanderful burst into tears. Her weight was the bane of her existence. Wanderful was five foot seven and weighed 183 pounds—eighty pounds more than the current fashion. When Wanderful first saw that "Just what you wear" Gap ad with the gamine woman in a ribbed, sleeveless vest and leggings, she considered moving to Antarctica. She knew she could never dress that way. Even worse, Wanderful had read in this magazine, and we're still apologizing to her, that those "Just what you wear" models who weigh 103 pounds are not anorexic. That in fact, according to us, they eat like horses. This was beyond depressing since when Wanderful ate like a horse she weighed 193 pounds.

But our editor was intrepid. "Please, I don't know anyone in Independence, and I was hoping we could have a cup of coffee."

Being a midwestern girl, Wanderful couldn't help but be hospitable. "Hi, my name is Wanda Knox," she said. "I'm sorry, this is a really bad night for me. My prom date got a flat tire, and now you want to know my weight."

"Since you have some spare time tonight, would you mind posing for a few pictures?"

Wanda had read *In Cold Blood* and knew that sometimes really weird things *did* happen in the Midwest.

"Are you sure you're on the level?" she asked.

"We can do it right here at Hardee's," our editor reassured her. "I only ask that if these photos come out the way I hope they will, you'll start using only one name."

"My boyfriend calls me Wandala like the *Sports Illustrated* swimsuit model. But that's just wishful thinking."

"Wanderful. We'll call you Wanderful. And after tonight no prom date is ever going to get a flat tire on you again."

That was the night hips and thighs returned to American couture in a big way. That was the night women without hanging flesh on their arms began wearing long-sleeved shirts. That was the night women in combat boots and leggings no longer looked like toothpicks on a tire, but rather like they could conquer the Ukraine. That was the night supermodel Wanderful gave birth to the bulge look.

That was just the beginning. By now everyone knows Bye-lorussia, the five-foot-four, 250-pound, blue-eyed cover girl whose signature style is flat shoes and elastic-waistband skirts; Katie McNally, the jeans queen, whose thighs are wider than her knees; and, of course, Dorothea, the African-American beauty who started the pinchable-cheeks rage.

Of course, some of our readers are outraged. We get angry letters like "After all these years of sharp angles, how do you expect us to grow curves and hips?" We know the bulge look makes thin women feel embarrassed about their flat tummies. High school students are not only wearing pads on their stomachs and hips but, in an overzealous effort to be fashionable, have begun gorging themselves on Heath Bar Crunch ice cream and duck sausage while avoiding exercise. Former supermodels like Naomi Campbell have stolen away to fat farms, where they binge on foie gras for two weeks.

Just as Kate Moss, Amber Valletta, Emma Balfour, Cecilia Chancellor—the waifs of the early nineties—were ectomorphic (naturally thin and not starving), so Wanderful, Byelo, Katie, and Dorothea are endomorphic and naturally curvaceous. They don't really gorge for their looks, and they certainly don't abstain from exercise. Most of the superbulges just eat when they're hungry and occasionally swim when on vacation. Of course, there is a popular assumption that these models stuff themselves, that they have regular lipo-insertions to round out their bodies. Both of these assumptions are false.

Calvin Klein, Isaac Mizrahi, and Donna Karan have confessed that they adore the new curves. They were each in their own way tired of straight lines and underwear passing for haute couture. They use Rubens and Renoir as inspiration now and are challenged by the new "womanliness" of the bulge. Kao Koa, the hottest young bulge designer, explains that "ever since the sixties, female fashion has been dictated by a male medieval ascetic aesthetic. In other words, the ideal woman looked like Grünewald's Christ. It's a challenge to think of women as lusty. For so many years lusty was synonymous with *obese*."

Yes, there is a very exciting revolution going on in fashion. Just as Wanderful cried every time she saw a "Just what you wear" Gap ad, now other women cry when they see Wanderful in her size-large Gap sweatshirt promotion with the caption "The hearty look I live in."

Wanderful wants to make it clear that she and the new superbulges are not hoping that all the waifs learn to loathe their bodies just as Wanda Knox in Independence did before the bulge look began. She is not encouraging high school students to become secret eaters or middle-aged women to have thigh implants. Billy de Berkowitz, M.D., of the Sonoma Institute of Eating Disorders says, "Eating disorders don't come from fashion. They are a dysfunction of dysfunction." In other words, the fact that thin women are unable to be happy with their well-toned bodies has nothing to do with the current bulge trend, but rather with their early childhoods.

We know fashion is in the eye of the beholder. Bringing back the bulge has merely broken a stereotype and deconstructed fashion a little further. That night in Independence, our editor wasn't hoping for women to hate their bodies. We aren't trying to pull the rug out from under self-confidence. What we are endorsing is revolution and change, which is what self-determination and liberation are all about. Besides, for the time being, bulge just looks better.

Making Nice:
When Is Enough Enough?

ast month I was voted Miss Colitis. I was honored at the Waldorf-Astoria and presented with a Steuben glass bowl by Mary Ann Mobley Collins, a former Miss America. It's not that the treatment of colitis is an unworthy mission, but I have no personal connection to the cause except that I received a letter from the Colitis Committee asking me to show up. In other words, I became Miss Colitis because I am very nice.

Whatever *nice* means, I've been it all my life. In second grade when the *New York Post* announced that William Zeckendorf, the very successful real estate developer, had fallen on hard times, I became unduly concerned about Mr. Z and his entire family. It wasn't as if I had ever met them—they certainly didn't run with my second-grade crowd. When I asked my father if the family Zeckendorf would be moving from their Park Avenue penthouse to a fifth-floor walk-up, he told me I'd be much more successful in life if I learned to worry more about myself. It horrifies me to think that if I were a child now I'd be weeping over the misfortunes of Trump's Taj Mahal.

I'm not exactly sure where my overwhelming drive to be

nice came from. Maybe it was from seeing *The Nun's Story* at an
early age and being impressed with the sister's commitment to
the Congo. I know I was never concerned about whether any
male heroes of mine, like the Beatles, John F. Kennedy, or
Hermann Hesse, were particularly nice. And I sort of always
had a secret thing for the Duke of Wellington and Shakespeare
because they probably weren't. But for me, being nice—plain
old accepting, decent nice—has always been the basic rule of
any social interaction. In other words, I'm the last person who
should be in charge of a totalitarian dictatorship.

Nice doesn't have to be drippy. It simply means no one's
ever said they were sorry to meet you. When a nice person
leaves the room, no one would ever mutter, "She's just horrible!" That's not drippy; that's a diplomatic and acrobatic feat
of enormous proportions. Being nice seemed, at least when I
was growing up, one of the good female qualities. It meant
being truly considerate, caring, and even believing that people
could connect for a purpose higher than self-aggrandizement.
Being nice meant that kindness was a virtue as opposed to a
naive miscalculation. The bad guys never worried about being
nice—or finishing last.

Recently I was on a panel discussing the future of the American theater—I should really join Good Causes Anonymous—
and an argument about the state of criticism became quite
heated. When the moderator said, "Let's ask Wendy what she
thinks," one of my fellow panelists lovingly but dismissively
remarked, "Oh, Wendy will never tell you. She's too nice." On
cue I smiled, giggled, twirled my hair, did all the dumb nice
things that I loathe that I do, as if to say, "Oh, yes, you're
right, I'm nice, so I don't have any opinions that really matter,
and you don't have to worry about me."

This is not to say that being nice isn't a virtue, which, like
all virtues, has a definite kickback. Katie Couric seems nice in

the best possible way: bright, hardworking, and personable. And frankly, my own niceness, a driving desire to be pleasant to every usher, concession-stand dealer, and ticket taker in the theater, has been very useful. Being nice, for me, has also allowed me to maintain a very pleasant distance. It's hard to get emotional or angry at someone who has just sent you a plant and, if she could, would throw in a co-op. I would just be being nice if I didn't say I've used my desire to please to the best possible advantage.

But the nice tables have turned. Nice is not very PC. Nice isn't an "in your face" kind of move. Nice doesn't stand up for what you believe in. Nice is wishy-washy, almost appallingly nonassertive, and definitely not very edgy. Demand an answer from any assertion technocrat, and she'll agree. Nice is very noblesse oblige, very unicultural. Nice only happens when someone can afford to be. Or even worse, nice underlines the unempowered; you're nice because you're not entitled not to be. Nice is very dated, very retro. It belongs on the shelf along with sugar and spice. And to top it all, nice isn't very sexy, it's certainly not dangerous, and it's too bland and forgiving for even a bimbo, which, by the way, isn't a very nice way to talk about a younger, attractive, differently talented woman. Frankly, as personal qualities go, nice is currently rated below good dental hygiene. A bumper sticker was sighted last week outside Cleveland: I'D RATHER FLOSS THAN BE NICE.

Lately, whenever I'm complimented for being nice, I know the choice was hideously wrong. For instance, when a man says, "You're a very nice woman," the rest of the sentence is, "but you're not my type." The longtime lover of one of my best men friends received a message from him extolling her for what a wonderful friend and nice person she had been recently. Two days later she learned that the same lover had left her— for another man. Of course, when my friend asked my advice about the incident, I suggested they all remain on good terms because life is short, and one doesn't make that many real connections. Sometimes I am ridiculously nice.

No one seems to care if Hillary Rodham Clinton, Janet Reno, Janet Jackson, or Barbra Streisand is nice. Difficult and demanding seem to be far more desirable. Barbra may or may not be nice, but her heart's in the right place, she's for the right causes, and I've even read somewhere that she watches C-SPAN. You don't get to sleep in the Lincoln Bedroom because you're nice. Nice will get you maybe to a bake-off, and that's valuable only if you can put a twist on a recipe for chocolate chip cookies. The only recent newsworthy woman who's come out of the spin cycle as "nice" is Tipper Gore, and she seems to have captured the public imagination about as much as her husband.

Being nice seems to have been replaced with striving for an abrasive right and wrong. If you believe in the correct things, oddly enough from the point of view of the right or the left, then you are entitled to drive your vision home. In other words, dialogue, a differing of opinion, is now almost as wishy-washy as being nice. Nice means there's a possibility of communication. Of course, there's no reason to communicate when the ultimate goal is to manipulate any opposition. Only gooey girls believe in conversation for conversation's sake. Real hard women, with bodies of steel, can squeeze any man, woman, or vegetable by the balls until they succumb and yell "Auntie!"

I choose to believe that Audrey Hepburn and Eleanor Roosevelt were actually sort of nice. I choose to believe they had a generous spirit that motivated their concerns for others. I choose to believe they could use their charms for what they believed in. But what they believed in also made them charming. I know that sometimes I've played my "niceness" to my advantage. I know that certain powerful men are apt to be more helpful to earnest daughter figures than to scheming semiotics majors from Brown in Azzedine Alaia tube dresses. I also know that women will often feel less competitive with a supposedly nice colleague than with a viper who eyes their office with a clear vision of redecorating. In other words, I'm not an innocent nice person. I've used my "niceness" many times, as I'm sure others have for centuries.

At times of my greatest moral dilemmas, I often consult the teachings of my mother, Lola Wasserstein—housewife, mother, and cancer extraordinaire—for guidance. On the subject of being nice, Lola Wasserstein makes two distinctions. According to her, "Sometimes it pays to be nice, and other times it's nice to be nice." What scares me is that right now it seems the only time it's all right to be nice is when it pays.

Next year when I get a call to be Miss Endometriosis, I'm going to try to just say no. And when a fellow panel member says I'm too nice to speak, I hope I wipe him right off the stage with my staggeringly acerbic bitchiness. If my friend's ex-lover invites her out for too many weekends with his new lover, I'll tell her that at some point she becomes a doormat, and that's not nice. That's just stupid. She'd be better off getting down, getting mean, getting angry.

I wouldn't mind shedding the nice part of me that gets me taken for granted or is trying far too hard to be likable. But on the other hand, I would hate to not still care if Mr. Zeckendorf lost all his money (ridiculous though that may sound). Frankly, I never want to leave a room and be thought of as a horrible person. I prefer to be someone who always sends a thank-you card or plant. Or maybe a co-op.

The State of the Arts

ooking back on my childhood, I would say that in many ways the arts saved my life. Well, if not *saved,* then gave it a shape and a purpose. Of course my parents never said to me, "Wendy darling, please, please grow up to be a not-for-profit theater writer. Whatever you do, we want you to have a life that is as financially insecure as possible, so please date actors, rely on the kindness of critics, and for heaven's sake don't have any reasonable health insurance."

However, when I was young my parents did send me to dancing school for the usual ballet and tap lessons, hoping that I would become well-rounded. (As far as I can make out, that well-roundedness went directly to the hips.) After dancing class, my folks and I would go, as they put it, "to take in a play." We saw an eclectic mix of Broadway and off-Broadway. I will never forget sitting in the front row with Morris and Lola at Edward Albee's *Seascape.* And it was when I was ten, during a performance of *No Time for Sergeants,* that I began to ask myself why there weren't any girls like me on stage.

At about the same time that my parents began taking me to the theater, my older sister Sandra began taking me to the New York City Ballet. We gasped at Edward Villella and

Jacques D'Amboise in *Apollo* and *Stars and Stripes*. Whereas adolescent life was chaos, in the ballet passion and exuberance were brilliantly contained. In fact, I still find the ballet one of the greatest solaces in life. In a world of brand names, image makers, and manipulated perceptions, the discipline and artistry of dance remind me that there is a form of human achievement that is unarguably and profoundly true.

I believe it is impossible to separate the arts from education. As a child I was diagnosed with a reading problem. Words in books flew around the room when I tried to read them. I was convinced that the "Fly to Europe" advertisements on the subway were actually offering tours to Ethiopia, and the spelling of "Coney Island" still baffles me. But at my elementary school there was a dancing teacher who took us to Prospect Park with a drum and called out colors as we danced. In retrospect it sounds like a Brooklyn version of Summerhill School, but at the time it was a true opportunity for exuberance and creativity. We also put on plays at school. Mini-versions of Shakespeare. I'll never forget my husband Caesar appearing in his mother's butterfly Martex sheets. And I can still play Felix Mendelssohn's score for *A Midsummer Night's Dream* on a triangle—though I'm not often asked to.

Most of the students from those early productions became something other than playwrights or actors. But we all learned that there exists a form of work in which people come together to create something which they deeply care about. We also learned discipline. If you rehearsed and studied your lines, ultimately you'd have more fun. For children, the arts are not simply icing on the cake. They are a way of including everyone in a joint, and joyous, venture. Moreover, the arts help children with unconventional study skills gain confidence in their uniqueness.

I am often asked how my first play was brought to the stage. Frankly, it came about because Lola was walking down the street one day and ran into Louise Roberts, the former secretary at the June Taylor School of Dance. Louise asked my mother, "How's Wendy?" Lola began hyperventilating. "Wendy isn't going to law school, she's not marrying a lawyer, and now she's writing plays!" Louise told her—probably to soothe my mother's spirits—that she was now in charge of a new not-for-profit dancing school called the Clark Center, which was across the hall from Playwrights Horizons at the Y on Eighth Avenue and Fifty-second Street. She said she would give Bob Moss, the artistic director of that theater, my play— a one-act ironically titled *Any Woman Can't*. Bob Moss agreed to produce a staged reading, and I have now been associated with Playwrights Horizons for twenty-five years.

I remember when Playwrights Horizons moved from the Y to Forty-second Street, into the former Maidman Playhouse. The Sex Institute of Technology was upstairs. We had a gala opening when Joan Mondale came to christen Theater Row. Nonprofit arts institutions are often pioneers in urban revival. The "new" Forty-second Street—the Disney-restored theaters and entertainment malls—would not be there today if the arts organizations sponsored by the National Endowment for the Arts and local arts councils had not taken the initiative to change the urban landscape.

In the mid-1990s I went to Washington, D.C., to lobby for individual grants to authors. I was part of a group called Poets and Writers, and with me were Melanie Griffith, Joanne Woodward, and the author Walter Mosley. At that time Jane Alexander, who had been on Broadway in *The Sisters Rosensweig,* was the chairwoman of the NEA, and the Speaker of the House, Newt Gingrich, refused to meet with her. It therefore sent ripples through the entire endowment when he agreed to dine with our visiting pro-arts delegation. At breakfast that morning, the Speaker told Melanie Griffith that if his novel was ever made into a film, he had two parts for her. During coffee I was asked to talk about my NEA grant. I mentioned that I had won a twelve-thousand-dollar grant in 1984, which had aided me in completing *The Heidi Chronicles*. In my mind, that's a small investment for a play that ran on Broadway for two years, toured the country for two years, and kept many people employed and inner cities lively. The Speaker looked up at me and said, "You know, Arthur Murray never needed a grant to write a play." Now, from my years of dancing school I know who Arthur Murray is. I even know that he ended all his television programs by advising his viewers to "put a little fun in your life: try dancing." But I kept quiet. I didn't want to jeopardize the funding. On the way out, after his aide whispered in his ear, the Speaker turned to me and said, "I'm terribly sorry. I meant Arthur Miller." I replied, "Yes. And he did have a grant. It was called the WPA."

That's a good story. But it's not as relevant as the one about the congressman I met that day who told me the arts are not as important an issue as education, because they are "elitist." Sure, his daughter loved her ballet class; but that didn't mean the government should fund it. The arts, he said, are extracurricular. Furthermore, they are no longer the popular culture. This attitude is far more disturbing to me than the Murray/Miller confusion.

Nonprofit arts in America are a thirty-seven-billion-dollar industry. We read statistics that opera is thriving and museum exhibits have given Jackson Pollock and van Gogh rock-star status. But if everything is really on the upswing, why are the arts still treated by many as an extracurricular activity—and therefore unworthy of serious support—rather than as a national priority? The year I won a Guggenheim grant for playwriting, I felt enormous pride—as if I had received a mandate to continue working. But when I called my father and told him about the eighteen-thousand-dollar grant, he said to me, "No daughter of mine is going on welfare!"

Even a grant with the distinguished reputation of a Guggenheim is a small amount of money compared with what a first-year lawyer or marketing researcher is paid. It reflects a question of priorities. How much do we value our artists? Are we giving them the message that to be successful they must find approval in the commercial arena? Has the word "elitist" crept in because the American public has been misled into believing that artists don't work for a living?

The arts, for all their strength, remain vulnerable. They are a constant source of politicization. The slightest whiff of controversy causes us to fear that funding will disappear. Anyone who speaks out about the NEA is inevitably asked about Mapplethorpe or Karen Finley. The hottest buttons seem to be about books and plays never seen by those who hold the most adamant opinions. Only if there is a clear-cut commitment to the arts can we actually have a dialogue. Instead, arts administrators are constantly forced to second-guess censors.

The arts profoundly reflect the most democratic credo, the belief in an individual vision or voice. Our popular culture, on the other hand—be it Hollywood or television—is based on a common denominator. When a movie previews, an audience votes on notecards as to whether they liked the ending. If they didn't, the producer will reshoot the film to try to fulfill audience expectation and therefore sell more tickets. By contrast, I distinctly remember an evening during a preview performance of *The Heidi Chronicles* when Joan Allen asked me if I'd mind if she substituted the word "a" for "the" in a certain speech. There is nowhere that the integrity of creation is respected more than it is in the arts. This belief in human potential gives both the audience and the creator pride in society's ability to nurture individuals.

Is it elitist not to search for a common denominator? Is it elitist to believe in an individual ability to craft talent? At a recent dinner, the eminent sociologist Robert Merton said to me: "Why is it that individual excellence is celebrated in sports but questioned in the arts? Why is it that we sit in awe of the basketball superstar Michael Jordan but believe that artists with similar outstanding talents should not be funded?" Why can't we celebrate the excellence of our artists without the undertow of elitism? There is no reason for our arts culture to be siphoned off to a marginal position from our national culture. No one wants to see the opera *Xerxes* every night, but no one wants to see *Lethal Weapon IV* every night, either. The truth is, the national culture is a texture of both. But that will become more and more one-sided unless we make the arts a part of the next generation of Americans' lives.

For every congressman who would say that the arts are elitist, I would answer that museums, plays, and dance are not responsible for violence in elementary schools or the tragedy at Columbine High or the hopelessness felt by many adolescents. If the solidity of the American family is changing and socioreligious structure is changing, one sure way for youngsters to find identity and commitment is through the arts. Ethics and morality, the question of how to live a decent life, are not dictated but rather most deeply explored in the arts.

There has never been more information available about weekend grosses, about how much money a movie star is getting for his or her next picture, about who Gwyneth Paltrow saw last night. But these are not the ideas that form the conscience of a nation. Or rather, if this kind of information is all we are happy to provide for the next generation, then we are engineering a depthless society with little ability to reason.

Character is not made by choices of fashion. In a world that endlessly celebrates the information revolution, the question of who will use that information must be answered.

It seems to me that on a very grassroots level, the survival of the arts in this country may have something to do with artists, playwrights, and dancers opening their world to the next generation. If a painter could take a group of DeWitt Clinton students to museums on a regular basis, if a dancer could take students in Chicago to performances, if a musician could take sophomores to concerts in Atlanta, we might on a fundamental level rebuild a constituency and eliminate the faulty concept of "elitism." There is nothing more inspiring for a student than to meet an artist who has managed to make a life of creation—whether the student goes on to become a playwright or simply learns to love the arts and think as an individual. And there's nothing more inspirational for an artist than being in touch with the future.

Perhaps it is finally time to celebrate excellence. To celebrate craft, discipline, ideas, and creation, and not get bogged down by those who oppose funding for the arts.

A national campaign cosponsored by a partnership of the entertainment industry and the not-for-profit arts agencies could vastly improve the image of the arts. The world of movies, television, graphic design, and high technology is fed by those of us who developed a specific voice or craft in the not-for-profit arena. There would be no *Lion King* if Julie Taymor had not found her vision in the not-for-profit arena. There would be no *Contact* (the Tony Award–winning musical) if Susan Stroman hadn't been able to develop her work at Lincoln Center Theater. *Angels in America* and *M. Butterfly* were both written by authors who received NEA grants. If the profit world is so enthused by such achievements, isn't it time they gave back to the initiators?

Once when I was advocating arts in the school, an educator asked me how I could possibly believe that the arts are more important than health or education. The arts, he argued, don't prepare students for well-paying careers. For a moment I felt like stammering, "What about the experience of taking pride in your own work? Isn't that vital to any career?" A society is defined by its culture, and that culture begins in early education. The decision to limit the arts is in fact what is elitist.

Finally, there must be a more creative form of subsidy. Recently I was at a dinner for the Guggenheim Foundation at which Vartan Gregorian and the novelist Michael Cunningham both said that receiving a grant from the Guggenheim Foundation had changed their lives. In other words, incentive goes a long way. If society won't support its artists, at least we can signal to them our hopes for their work and our support. Being an artist is an incredibly lonely job. Having an incentive for continuing to work is one way to keep a community if not fully subsidized, then at least recognized. The arts remain the true arena in which an individual can fearlessly look at the world and say, "Here's where we're going." The NEA and the WPA were innovative visions. As we move into the next century, it's time to strategize a funding coalition of profit and nonprofit. If the national culture is a texture of popular and high art, shouldn't the funding be as well? The arts—our society's benchmark—and the popular culture are separating. It's our challenge to bring them back together.

The task for all of us is to give the next generation of artists and Americans a chance to find and define the character of this nation. In a country so profoundly dedicated to the individual vision and freedom of interpretation, the potential is both magnificent and essential.

Dear Broadway,
This Isn't Really Goodbye

The night my play *The Heidi Chronicles* opened on Broadway, I was waiting for an experience similar to the one described by Moss Hart in his theatrical memoir, *Act One.* Mr. Hart had a lifelong dream of getting to Broadway. On the opening night of *Once in a Lifetime,* his fondest wish both as a New Yorker and as a man of the theater came true.

I am from a generation of off-Broadway babies. Unlike Mr. Hart, we mostly don't dare dream of getting our plays to Broadway now. Broadway in the past decades generally houses three or four new plays a year, one of which is often British.

Our plays, even the most well known, like A. R. Gurney's *The Dining Room* or Alfred Uhry's *Driving Miss Daisy,* have never been on Broadway. They have long and healthy lives in regional theaters across the country and in two-hundred- or three-hundred-seat commercial houses in New York, Chicago, or Los Angeles.

But the day I first walked, as an author, into the Plymouth, I became suddenly envious of Moss Hart and his theatrical era, when at times more than two hundred new American plays were produced on Broadway every year. As I sat in the empty orchestra while Daniel Sullivan, our director, and Thomas Lynch, the set designer, evaluated the sight lines, I thought it was the most beautiful and enormous theater I had ever seen.

I stared at the delicate gray and white rococo ceiling and wondered what John Barrymore, Laurette Taylor and even William Gillette, who opened in the theater in 1917, first thought when they gazed at it. Bernard Jacobs of the Shubert Organization tells me the Plymouth is his shining jewel, the most beautiful theater in New York—maybe, he says, even in America. I think it is in the world.

During the year and a half that my play has been fortunate to be at the Plymouth, I have never missed an opportunity to visit there. I've attended understudy auditions and cast-change rehearsals, and sometimes just came by during a matinee to pace in the back. In fact, what has amazed me as a New Yorker is that the lore of the theater district is still intact. It has been sadly scaled down, but is still intact.

For example, for a Broadway playwright there remains the thrill of the stage doorman knowing your name. I've never missed an opportunity to just say "Hi" to Richard White and Andrew Capps at the Plymouth. Conversely, the Plymouth ushers have never missed an opportunity to tell me their opinions on every cast change, and they're generally right. And I've come to rely on the anecdotes of "Broadway Ernie," Ernie Austin, our prop man, who has been an actor, singer, dancer, and stage manager and now has been doing Broadway props for twenty-five years.

My friend the late Edward Kleban, who wrote the lyrics for *A Chorus Line,* told me shortly before he died, "Kiddo, the thing about having a show on Broadway is you'll always have a private rest room in the theater district." As it turned out, Ed had the longest-running rest room in musical theater history.

It breaks my heart that I won't be regularly visiting with Roy Harris, our stage manager, in Lily Tomlin's and Maggie Smith's old dressing room. I've told Roy I think the Shubert Organization should change the theater's name to "Roy Harris's Plymouth Theatre" with Roy's hand waving in neon above.

But what I will miss the most is simply being inside the Plymouth Theatre. On Labor Day weekend in 1989, the original cast gave their final performance of my play in the afternoon and the new cast was to rehearse for the first time that night. After the actors packed up their dressing rooms and departed, the director and I went out to dinner. Eighth Avenue was abandoned except for men in white space uniforms. Though later we found out this was due to an asbestos pipe break, it seemed to us the end of the world. What to do seemed simple: Go back inside the Plymouth Theatre and put in the new company.

I have wondered often since that time how many New Yorkers would choose to go to the theater if it were indeed the end of the world. And I suspect the answer is quite a few. Even in a theatrical climate now beleaguered by censorship, soaring ticket prices, and embattled unions, theater is a New Yorker's sublime obsession: other towns have stages; we've got Broadway.

As I sat for the last time in the empty Plymouth Theatre, staring again at that gorgeous ceiling, I felt a true sadness that all Broadway theaters are not presently occupied with playwrights having the epiphany of Moss Hart. Moreover, my concern is that for future generations of playwrights, the Broadway epiphany will be the odd exception. It should be their legacy.

Poles Apart

Growing up, I always loved the stories about my mother's childhood. Lola's Poland was different from anybody else's mother's Poland. My schoolmates had grandfathers who were peddlers in Lodz, but my mother's family had a summer villa in a spa resort called Ciechocinek. My mother's family was the intelligentsia. At least according to my mother.

The stories got even better as I got older. My grandfather Shimon Schleifer, who was in fact a district school principal in Włocławek and an amateur playwright, emerged in family lore by the time I got to college as the first Polish Neil Simon, Martin Buber, and, if things had been different, Henry Kissinger. Frankly, I always placed the truth of the summer villa right alongside my mother's sworn testimony to me in eighth grade that grown women would pay thousands of dollars for hair like mine, especially when it divided into thousands of damaged, frizzy split ends. It might have been more than a slight exaggeration, but it was certainly comforting.

I would have happily passed on to the next generation the tale of Ciechocinek as the Polish Hamptons if Citibank had not decided to sponsor the New York Philharmonic's trip to

Warsaw. My sister Sandra, in her capacity as senior officer for corporate affairs at the bank, was meeting the orchestra there, and she asked me to join her earlier for a sisterly tour of our mother's Polish girlhood.

According to my mother, when she and her family got off the boat in New York, her Uncle Louis's chauffeur, the first African-American my mother ever saw, was waiting in a stretch limo to greet her. When Sandra and I arrived in Warsaw more than sixty years later, our chauffeur Jimmy and his Mercedes were waiting to meet us. Driving into downtown Warsaw, one is immediately struck by the number of cars and the liveliness of the pedestrians. The Warsaw women in their midi-length coats and berets and young Poles in blue jeans and bright ski parkas have a tempo and texture in direct contrast to the row after row of concrete "we shall bury you with drabness" Soviet prefabricated apartment houses. However, as we pull onto Jerozolimskie, one of the main thoroughfares, the bright lights of capitalism are twinkling even at ten o'clock in the morning.

Pizza Hut, DRINK COCA-COLA, and two, count them two, McDonald's are all heralding the new world order. In downtown Warsaw there are no Workers for Freedom posters, no Marxist-Leninist topiary, no pioneer children parading in red scarves for a better tomorrow. However, the pièce de résistance of Stalinist Polish architecture, the Palace of Culture and Science, remains in the center of the city as a living monument to the recently deposed past. But the present and the future Poland is just across the street at the all-faxing, all-direct-international-dialing Hotel Marriott.

The Warsaw Marriott is a crossroads for the new Eastern Europe, East meets West on the banks of the Vistula. Concierges named Magda and Inge sporting Hillary Rodham Clinton headbands eagerly recommend the hot spots for "nouvelle Polish cuisine." At the Chicago Steakhouse, Poles in the latest leather midiskirts order sirloins while Eric Clapton takes them to Muzak heaven.

My sister and I have arranged for Jimmy to take us on the Lola Schleifer Wasserstein Freedom Trail. We will drive north along the Vistula to Włoclawek, site of our mother's Winter Palace, and then on to Ciechocinek. Jimmy, who is around thirty, was a full-time merchant marine during the previous world order, and these days for extra cash he moonlights as a driver and interpreter. As we leave the city, Jimmy drives us past the residence of the former Communist head of state, General Jaruzelski. As far as Jimmy, the military man, is concerned, something has been lost as well as gained in the transition to the new Poland. In other words, Lech Walesa may have eleven children, but he is no general.

Weeping willows in the Polish countryside are trimmed back in the early spring practically to their trunks. Driving along the single-lane highway past the lovely brick farmhouses, one imagines the armies of Swedes, Prussians, Germans, and Russians who alternately ravaged and staked claim to these gentle lands. Driving along with my big sister, who knew my grandfather Shimon, I imagine his escape through this countryside north to Gdansk, and his remaining friends and their families being herded like cattle on this road for the final solution.

Włoclawek has been the seat of the Polish bishop in the Kujawy province since the middle of the twelfth century. Jews were prohibited from settling in the town until the eighteenth century. My mother's childhood memories are slightly fuzzy. After all, she left the country at age twelve. But according to her big brother, Henry, they grew up in a cream-colored building with a veranda on Piekarska Street, and my mother recalls strolling with her housekeepers. It is a grim industrial town, with a huge paper mill graying now from the national scourge of air pollution. Włocławek is now best known in Poland for producing glazed porcelain, hand-painted with a brown floral motif. My mother, who is not averse to displaying a tchotchke or two, never had brown floral porcelain in her places of honor. She is, however, very prone to the same white lace curtains one sees in almost every window in Poland, from Włocławek to Warsaw. They are, in fact, hanging this very night in her bedroom on the Upper East Side of Manhattan.

When we find Piekarska Street it is indeed two blocks away from the Vistula, near a lovely park surrounding a fourteenth-century church. Jimmy explains to us that "Poland is a country of churches." My sister and I smile and nod in agreement. "Your mother must have been very well-to-do," he continues. "Only the very well-to-do lived in corner houses."

My sister and I smile again. We have no idea if Jimmy has put together the fact that neither of us is wildly enthusiastic about the Polish churches. For two big talkers, my sister and I don't offer Jimmy any specific information. My sister is a formidable banker, and I am a playwright. But today we are two Jewish girls in Poland. It's not exactly comfortable to speak.

We drive north to Ciechocinek, passing the turnoff to Gdansk. My grandfather left Poland unexpectedly in the mid-1920s. He was at a café on the town square in Włocławek with his intelligentsia friends, discussing all the latest isms—socialism, atheism, Zionism—when a pal arrived to say the police were on their way. It seems the Polish police were not as impressed with the ideologies of the twentieth century as Shimon Schleifer was. My grandfather never went home again. Instead, he went directly to Gdansk, a free port, got a message to his wife, and weeks later went on to America with a false Greek passport. Two years later my mother and the rest of her family were met at the New York pier by my Uncle Louis's chauffeur. Only my mother's sister Hela, who had recently fallen in love and married, remained in Poland. She and her family died in the camps.

Ciechocinek remains a resort town. Past the obligatory cinder-block buildings are lovely parks, gardens in bloom, and even the bandstand where my mother first danced. According to my mother, wherever she lived, wherever she danced, wherever she ate, was the best place to live, the best place to dance, and the best place to eat. The Miller Hotel, decayed now, is still standing, as is the Bristol Cafe, an almost-grand Tudor structure that still serves refreshments and ice cream. Today in Ciechocinek there are still the parks and even the famous spa water, but no one looks like my sister or me. No one even resembles the women from my mother's faded photo album. Fifty years ago the ethnic cleansing of Ciechocinek was so successful that there is no variety here. Everyone looks pretty much the same.

The following morning Jimmy takes us on a tour of Greater Warsaw. He turns down the road into the Muranow district and again we pass row after row of cinder-block housing and early spring trees. "This is the site of the Warsaw Ghetto. In the 1940s half a million Jews from all over Poland lived here."

The Muranow district of Warsaw seems as likely a ten-block radius of a ghetto as Queens, New York, or downtown Houston. The past, the uprising, the life behind the walls of the Nazi-designed ghetto, have completely vanished except for the Ghetto Heroes Monument, unveiled in 1948. The half million—the largest minority group in all of Poland—who were sent to the camps are marked in memory by a simple tablet. Just as McDonald's now erases fifty years of Communism, the gray cinder block subdues from memory the horror of the Holocaust. It is terrifyingly successful.

My sister and I bid farewell to Jimmy and take a taxi to the

Nozyk Synagogue, the only remaining synagogue in Warsaw. It is one week before the fiftieth anniversary of the ghetto uprising. When we finally arrive, the synagogue doors are locked, but there is a swastika spray-painted on the front doors: JUDEN RAUS. I take my big sister's hand.

I took a Lufthansa flight from Warsaw to London, the only woman on a plane full of German businessmen. I was looking forward to a glass of wine and a good private stare at the clouds as my eyes would tear for my mother, Shimon, and the past. But my journey wasn't sentimental until the flight attendant came around with the *Herald Tribune.* While I was in the sky, the Serbian leader Milosevic, the man who reinvented ethnic cleansing for the nineties, was at the UN defending his position in Bosnia and Herzegovina. And as I read the well-thought-out explanations of why other nations could or could not intervene, I began to cry. Perhaps fifty years from now in Bosnia and Herzegovina everyone will look exactly the same.

In the Passover Haggadah the young child is told that every year he must retell the story of Passover, and every year he must think of himself as a Jew leaving Egypt. The stories of Włocławek, Ciechocinek, and the Warsaw Ghetto must be told, or they will become like those cinder-block apartment complexes: characterless, displaced, concealing—and therefore accepting—unbearable evil.

Ah, That First Feast
in Wild Manhattan

was very disappointed the first time I saw Plymouth Rock. There it was, just a rock. Somehow I was hoping for more of a to-do. I thought that rock would be surrounded by Barricini chocolate turkeys, dancing sweet potatoes, and Pilgrims in crepe-paper hats singing "We gather together to ask the Lord's blessing."

But then Thanksgiving has always been my favorite family production. We didn't live over the river and through the woods but on the Upper East Side of Manhattan. Our mother never boiled cranberries for hours. She dialed the takeout department of Cooky's restaurant. So for me, the first Pilgrims' landing left a great deal to the imagination.

Actually, my favorite Thanksgiving was my family's first feast after we sailed across the East River from our house in Flatbush, Brooklyn, and landed in a modern Lexington Avenue white wedding-cake-tiered apartment building. This was in the mid-sixties, when the latest look in city living was "walk-in," or rather "walk-through," kitchens and L-shaped living-dining-room areas. It had all the glamour of a hotel effi-

ciency and none of the services. The previous tenant of our new
apartment was Ann Sothern of *Private Secretary* fame, who had
removed all the standard doors and replaced them with double
French numbers. So although there was no room to cook or
even stand in the kitchen, you could make quite a theatrical
entrance!

Dining room or dining area, as far as my mother was concerned, Thanksgiving was meant for family. As far as we four
children were concerned, family meant not only siblings but
all of our extended friends. After all, if you were lucky enough
to grow up in New York, why wouldn't you want to show
it off? For years, over Thanksgiving holidays we were enter-
taining college roommates who had never been on a subway
before, to the city before, or even slept in an apartment before.

That Thanksgiving when we had just moved, I believe my
older brother brought home at least five friends from his college newspaper, the *Michigan Daily*. I tripped over Harvey
Wasserman in a sleeping bag in the living room, and Clarence
(Flash) Fanto was neatly tucked away on two chairs with a
sheet over him in the dining room. I suppose it would have
been more convenient if they had taken over my room, but
even my mother's generosity had its boundaries.

Planning a family meal for twenty had its challenges, but
my mother was always at the forefront of takeout culinary art.
But because we were new in the neighborhood, she wasn't
familiar with the local talents to dial. So she and my father
went back to basics. They drove an hour to Cooky's on Avenue
M in Brooklyn to pick up Thanksgiving for twenty to go. My
parents were smuggling cranberry sauce and potato kugel over
interborough lines.

This unusual catering service continued over the next ten
years. She never bothered to get the obvious numbers in Man-

hattan. Every Thanksgiving when my sister and her family would arrive from Vermont, my mother would already have unpacked all the catering, hidden away the foil and the Tupperware, and be busy boiling garlic to create that real down-home Lexington Avenue atmosphere. On entry, every year, my brother-in-law the doctor would say, "Lola, it smells delicious!" And she would so graciously reply: "Of course it does. I've been cooking for hours!"

When all the Barricini chocolate turkeys are in place and my family finally sits down to Thanksgiving dinner, from that very first one in Manhattan to the ones now, at least four generations are around the table. I will never forget my father in his maroon smoking jacket beaming at his first grandchild, who was inevitably squeezed between two of my brother's college roommates. I will never forget my mother announcing to my college roommate, Mary Jane Patrone of Glenview, Illinois, "I pass the gravy to my children!" Later, when I asked Mary Jane if she had found it all bizarre, she said she loved belting "The Turkey Ran Away Before Thanksgiving Day" ("Said he, 'They'll make a roast out of me if I should stay' ") with my entire family on Lexington Avenue.

My parents now have nine grandchildren, two of whom were born right after Thanksgiving—maybe it was my mother's cooking. My eldest niece is now older than my brother was at that first Thanksgiving in Manhattan. We don't have the family holiday in my mother's L-shaped dining area anymore; we have it in my big sister's prewar formal Madison Avenue dining room. And my sister cooks—both a ham and a turkey!

But we still all sing "The Turkey Ran Away." We still decorate with chocolate turkeys. My niece arrived last year with a girl she met in Italy who had never been in New York before.

For old times' sake, my mother even brings over a takeout potato kugel and we still compliment her on her cooking and ask for the recipe. This year I will give thanks that, like the Pilgrims, our family managed to make such a good life on the rock where we landed.

New York Theater:
Isn't It Romantic

There is a new phenomenon in New York. Every night at seven-thirty hordes of eager diners pour out of restaurants, from the intimate French bistros of Greenwich Village to the 874-seat "Only Guacamole" Yuppeterias on the Upper West Side. Across Manhattan former "foodies" are forfeiting a final mousse and leaving a soufflé flat. But where is everybody going? To the theater, of course.

"Everyone's life simply revolves around curtain time, my dear," whispered a discreet trendsetter at a discreet Madison Avenue salon. "I had Henry, V.S., Tama, Paloma, Ved, Cyrus, and Kiri to dinner the other night. And all they talked about were new American plays! I tried to steer the conversation around to film, or even Reykjavík, but they wouldn't hear of it. The theater is at the top of everybody's To Do list."

And the cultural exodus is not just from restaurants. The entire city of London is empty in the summer. British tourists are flocking to New York to see American plays and musicals. They just can't wait until next year's transfer to the West End. Every other person in the Broadway audience has an English accent.

The renewed vitality of the New York theater has caused some hard rethinking at diverse social gathering spots such as discotheques, bowling alleys, and video shoppes. Seminars on topics like "Are Videocassettes Dying?" and "How to Make a Living with Sun-Dried Tomatoes" are being held in the meeting rooms formerly occupied by annual "Is Broadway dying?" and "How to Make a Living in the Theater" symposiums.

"It's a wonderful thing in life to be able to make a living at what you really want to do," a New York playwright was overheard saying while encouraging an undergraduate to apply to drama school over business school. In this period of renewed theatrical activity, off-Broadway and regional theater are able to commission plays with fees to the writer equal to those paid to any television scripter. Moreover, because of the audience's insatiable appetite for new plays, a single review can't make or break anything. Audiences and critics have a commitment to the long-term career of the playwright; the old hit-or-miss conditions no longer apply. In fact, parents now consider playwriting a secure profession.

Not since the farmer and the cowboy became friends have so many drama critics, from all fifteen daily newspapers, sought out the community of playwrights. Mutual respect and appreciation of divergent visions is a given. It's not uncommon for noted drama critics to publish a revised opinion after a stimulating give-and-take with an author. Conversely, a Broadway choreographer may restage a number in the midst of a successful run after a conversation with a critic.

Yes, we've all become a family. "We just want to do more plays," a higher-up at Actors' Equity chirped to a member of the Society of Stage Directors and Choreographers at a Dramatists Guild dance. "I see myself as an environmentalist," confessed a tough union negotiator. "All theatrical unions are desperately concerned with preserving an environment in which our art can flourish."

A recent lunch at Orso's is indicative of the prosperity of the current theater flowing into the surrounding community. The atmosphere was jubilant. The Broadway titans, the Nederlanders and the Shubert Organization, toasted Curt Dempster of the Ensemble Studio Theatre, André Bishop of Playwrights Horizons, Lynne Meadow of the Manhattan Theatre Club, and Joseph Papp. They noted that in the 1985–86 season 560 new American plays and musicals opened in New York, and vowed that next year they'd join forces to beat that record. The mood was so ecstatic that Mr. Papp offered to divide the Public Theater's profits from *A Chorus Line* with every not-for-profit theater in the city. "It's as much yours as mine," he cried. The Shuberts, amid the elation, scheduled a one-act marathon at the Morosco Theatre. It sold out immediately!

Actors' agents quickly caught on to the trend and began cautioning their clients about accepting work in television and film. "Sure, do a movie from time to time for a stretch. But hold out for a play" became the passwords in the halls of International Creative Management and the William Morris Agency. Casting directors for television situation comedies have been forced to turn to real-life single women and actual wise-cracking teenagers because the professional talent is not available. Ninety-five percent of the members of Actors' Equity are working on the New York stage.

Looking back now, most audiences can't remember why they stopped coming to the theater to begin with. A random sampling recalls growing up on *My Fair Lady* and *Gypsy* and that chill of anticipation when the houselights go down. Others say they have always enjoyed opera, dance, music, but that it doesn't replace the spoken word. And young theatergoers who make the trip every year to Brooklyn to the Next Wave Festival consider it all a matter of attitude. For them, the attitude at a theater devoted to new works is not just hip but refreshingly sequential.

But why the sudden reversal? Why now? Was it that the situation had become so bleak that it just had to turn around? Was it all caused by the "Death of the Theater" panel at which all the producers, for profit and not, wore black, and a casket full of playbills lay on the podium? Was it the Hollywood press release that after the joint movie studio takeover of Broadway, all playwrights would be forced to submit treatments or outlines for their plays, with the possibility of being fired before the first draft? Or was it the Yale School of Drama's imminent decision to relocate in beautiful downtown Burbank?

Yes, there were dire rallying signs. But there were silent fears, too. The fear that all corporate and government funding for the arts would dry up. The fear that the best stage actors were, understandably, being advised to "hold out for pilot season." The fear that all those "whither the theater" articles were true. And finally, the most personal fear that the art we create has the societal place of stained glass—glorious, but past its heyday. But think positively.

Let's begin small. Perhaps it was returning to affordable ticket prices that brought the audience back. As soon as the theater became cheaper than an evening with a free-range chicken, the box-office phones began ringing. The reclaimed vitality of the theater district, a play in every house, produced without the cost of mortgaging one's mother-in-law, brought the producers back. And the rumor that Ron Darling, the now-former Mets pitcher, had at one time written a play helped bring the writers back. And the writers brought the directors, the actors, and the designers back.

That was all encouraging, but I'd say it was simpler. Those

of us who work in the theater all wanted to be here. When we dream, we dream of dialogue, lights, cues, house laughs, ovations, and sight lines. We don't dream about deal memos, and cueing the *Starship Enterprise.* None of us do. We learn to do it well. But we don't dream about it.

Those of us who work in the theater work in a live art form. We don't produce stained glass. It was the theater's endurance as the great art form of the individual voice that brought all of us back. The turnabout took a concerted effort, from playwrights, producers, actors, designers, technicians, agents, lawyers, critics, and audiences. But it was all worth it.

A few weeks ago a crowd of well over fifty thousand people at Shea Stadium cheered to see, among others, Meryl Streep, Bill Moor, Mary Alice, Kevin Kline, Chip Zien, David Alan Grier, Nancy Marchand, Alma Cuervo, Christine Estabrook, Peter Evans, James Earl Jones, William Hurt, Fisher Stevens, Jonathan Hogan, Michelle Shay, Bernadette Peters, Olympia Dukakis, Anna Thompson, E. Katherine Kerr, and Rex Robbins in a World Series Evening of new and old American plays and musicals entitled "Night of a Thousand Stage Stars."

The plays included works by Christopher Durang, Arthur Miller, Charles Fuller, Betty Comden, Adolph Green, Lanford Wilson, Tina Howe, Gus Edwards, Neal Bell, Peter Parnell, Samm-Art Williams, Kevin Heelan, Bill Finn, Terrence McNally, Evan Smith, Marsha Norman, José Rivera, Albert Innaurato, Michael Weller, Robert Anderson, George C. Wolfe, Len Jenkin, Stephen Sondheim, and Cy Coleman. The evening was directed by George Abbott, James Lapine, Jerry Zaks, Peter Sellars, Oz Scott, Amy Saltz, Gerald Gutierrez, Mary Robinson, Lloyd Richards, Ellie Renfield, Mike Nichols, and Richard Foreman and produced by the Second Stage, the Shubert Organization, the Paper Bag Players, EST, WPA, Playwrights Horizons, the Manhattan Theatre Club, the Negro

Ensemble Company, the Nederlanders, Francine Lefrak, La MaMa, T. Edward Hambleton, Lincoln Center, and Lucille Lortel.

After a twenty-minute standing ovation in the rain, the audience leaped onto the field in unheralded excitement. An instantaneous ticker-tape parade followed the actors from the stadium to Times Square. It was "Amazin.' " (A dream come true.)

And best of all, the *New York Times* renamed the Arts & Leisure section the "Drama" section.

Directing 101:
George Abbott on What Works

George Abbott believes a director wastes his time in rehearsal when he talks endlessly to an actor about who his mother was, what did she want, what does he want, and why it has led him up to this moment when he asks for the salt. Instead he prefers that the director get on with it and tell the actor, "C'mon Johnny, just pass the salt." And for the last sixty years no one has known how to get Johnny on and off an American stage better than George Abbott.

"Do you want me to sit now, Mr. Abbott?" an actor turns upstage to ask the director. It's a familiar question. The other day, however, the question was being posed not on Broadway, where Mr. Abbott made his directing debut in 1926 with "Love 'Em and Leave 'Em," but rather in the basement of the Church of the Heavenly Rest at 2 East Ninetieth Street on Manhattan's Upper East Side. There Mr. Abbott is currently rehearsing *Frankie,* a new musical version of Frankenstein, for which he has also written the book. The musical began performances Friday at the off-off-Broadway theater, which occupies the day school gymnasium upstairs.

Though the locale has altered, Mr. Abbott's technique has not. The 101-year-old director remains in control of every line and every gesture on the stage. As he sits between his current collaborators, his codirector Donald Saddler and the composer Joseph Turrin, one can easily imagine previous teams in similar situations creating such George Abbott–directed classics as *The Pajama Game, On Your Toes,* and *Damn Yankees.*

Within minutes of the rehearsal's commencement, Mr. Abbott claps his hands to halt the action. From his chair, he meticulously directs every moment. When the monster Frankenstein enters the room, Mr. Abbott tells a supporting player, "Turn toward him and keep looking at him and say, 'Who's that?' In other words, as if you are asking, 'Is that a social friend?' "

What is fascinating for a playwright like myself, who was reared in a theater in which an actor's "process"—the search for motivation and character—is a primary part of rehearsals, is to watch Mr. Abbott's actors accept direction such as "Why don't you gesture here" or "Look at him and turn upstage there." A line reading from a director at most rehearsals these days could provoke a mutiny or at least a wail about the actor's "journey." But this company seems to have complete respect for their master craftsman. And every gesture, every line reading, seems to clarify the play and the performances.

George Abbott has been a mentor and inspiration to Hal Prince, Jerry Zaks, Gerald Gutierrez, and generations of American directors. Mr. Abbott's own early mentor was George Pierce Baker, the venerable playwriting professor at Harvard who, when Harvard refused to create a drama major, founded the Yale Drama School. Mr. Abbott credits Mr. Baker with teaching him that "any kind of writing for the theater is as good as anything else. In other words, a farce is just as good as a melodrama as long as you get the greatest good out of the scene."

Mr. Baker's advice is apparent in the span of Mr. Abbott's theatrical career. His accomplishments range from directing *A Tree Grows in Brooklyn* to the musical *A Funny Thing Happened on the Way to the Forum*. As Mr. Abbott more simply puts it, "I just like to work. It's fun."

His early contribution to the theater even included auditions. Apparently actors in his early days were hired based on a personal meeting and often fired the next day after the director heard them read the part. Equity, the actors' union, rightfully disapproved of this erratic behavior, and so Mr. Abbott conceived of the idea of having actors meet a director and read from the play being cast. Previous to Mr. Abbott, in other words, there were no casting calls, callbacks, or prepared comic-tragic-three-minute speeches. No wonder these actors take his line readings. They owe him a lot.

The stage manager of *Frankenstein* calls out "Halt!" as Mr. Abbott claps his hands again. The action stops, and the actors look up at their director. "Victor," Mr. Abbott says to Richard White, who is playing Frankenstein's naive inventor (Mr. Abbott always calls actors by the characters' names. He tells me it's old age that keeps him from remembering their real names. I tell him I can't remember either; it's middle age). "When you take the girl, you should . . ." He pauses. "I'll show you." For the first time during the rehearsal Mr. Abbott rises from his chair to put his arm around Elizabeth Walsh, who plays the good doctor's love interest.

For a moment I am reminded of Kitty Carlisle Hart's stories about going dancing with George Abbott. I imagine them elegantly sweeping across the floor in a previous theatrical era. Mr. Abbott acknowledges that he would always choose a partner who was a good dancer over "just a beauty." In fact, one of the triumphs of his long and distinguished career was a masquerade party in Havana where all the young women thought he was Cuban because of his expert Latin rhythms.

In the theater, a world of subjective make-believe, George Abbott has always been assumed to have the answers. But when asked about the fabled "show doctor" story in which he reportedly arrived at a three-act preview of Harold Prince's *Cabaret* and left with the simple dictum, "Two acts," Mr. Abbott modestly replied, "I know Hal says so. But I don't remember." To a playwright there is something very comforting about a director who can simply sit still and, in the midst of cascading action, clap his hands and utter, "Two acts." All playwrights are awaiting a second-act messiah.

Mr. Abbott's *Frankenstein* is a two-act musical—well, almost an operetta—that updates the familiar monster story. The action has moved from Transylvania to contemporary Westchester, and the doctor's brother is afraid that Victor's experiments will ruin the family's reputation at the country club.

As I watch the legendary director at this off-off-Broadway company where the scenery flats are being painted upstairs, I wonder what Mr. Abbott thinks about the current state of the American theater.

"Well, it's all quite different," Mr. Abbott explains to me. "Except it's the same. Wherever you are you go through various stages of progress toward a finished show. For instance, now we're rewriting, as we always do." Mr. Abbott is a man who holds on to the present and future, not the past.

It's impossible not to ask a man like Mr. Abbott which of his many plays and musicals is his favorite. And his answer is perhaps the key to his craft, his art, and his idea of theater. "I'd say," he says, "the last one. Your heart and your love go out to what you're working on now and your hopes for it."

Mr. Abbott claps his hands again. He nips a moment in the bud. "Now don't think you're funny," he tells an actor in a comic role. "It'll never work if you think it's funny." I write down the direction. I will try not to forget it. The advice is clear, precise, and in control.

When I leave, I ask Mr. Abbott if he has any specific thought for playwrights. Yes, he does. It is simply "Write." Mr. Abbott does not give this advice lightly. He's already working on a new piece.

Theater Problems?
Call Dr. Chekhov

There's a popular story going around the theatrical community in Los Angeles. Apparently a casting director called a Hollywood agent about setting up an audition for his client in a local production of *Three Sisters* and the agent efficiently queried, "Will the playwright be present at the audition?" Furthermore, the actor received notice of his audition by a routine message from the agent's secretary on his phone machine: "David, you're up for a part in *Sisters*. I'll have a messenger send over the script."

Now here the story diverges. Some say the agent urged the actor to take the part because being in plays offers high visibility during pilot season. Others claim that the agent preferred that the actor hold out for a guest shot on *Cagney & Lacey*. Where all versions agree, however, is that the actor, a man trained in the theater, was appalled. The reason is simple. For all of us who love the theater, Chekhov is the standard. Yes, Shakespeare is great, and Beckett is brilliant, and Ibsen the estimable craftsman, but Chekhov is beloved. Chekhov is who we reach for.

But plays do not have such longevity merely because they

are admired by men and women who work in the theater. Chekhov's plays begin with character and story, and therefore have remained universally appealing. A few years ago there was a production of *Three Sisters* at the Manhattan Theatre Club featuring Dianne Wiest, Mia Dillon, and Lisa Banes. During a visit to my parents' home, my mother told me she wanted to get tickets to this play about three Russian sisters who aren't married and come from a very nice family. Now, my mother wasn't interested in comparing the production to the Moscow Art Theatre, or in following Miss Wiest's rising theatrical career, though she would have been impressed that the playwright was a doctor. The truth was she was intrigued by the story. For her it seemed clearly a play about recognizable people.

The Chekhov plays are not snippets of lives. They have the richness, the canvas, of novels. The rise of the acquisitive sister-in-law Natasha in *Three Sisters,* is emblematic of a changing world. So is the advent of Lopakhin, the son of a peasant turned landlord in *The Cherry Orchard,* which is now being revived at the Brooklyn Academy of Music's Majestic Theater under the direction of Peter Brook. Chekhov is a master of time. How it advances. How it damages. That is more than an ambitious theatrical sweep. That's greatness. But I'm getting pretentious, and the key to Chekhov is he is never pretentious. He is always human. Perhaps, therefore, I am fortunate that I first came across his plays naively, even obliquely. When I was a first-year student at Yale Drama School and absorbed in my own artistic and personal ennui, my schoolmate, the playwright Christopher Durang, suggested that I read *Three Sisters.* Immediately I became obsessed with the play. On days when I couldn't decide what to do after graduate school, I would repeat to myself again and again the Prozorov sisters' familiar "I must go to Moscow. I must go to Moscow."

Soon I was relating all my life to Chekhov. The future of a family property was suddenly *The Cherry Orchard*. I wondered which classmates of mine were Nina, the impressionable would-be actress in *The Seagull,* and which of us writers would grow up to be her Trigorin, well known and never pushed beyond our limits. At that time I tried to see every Chekhov production I could, student, professional, Equity, Equity waiver. My particular favorite was a Grotowski-influenced production at Harvard of *Three Sisters* in which the cast and audience sang and danced to the Beatles' "Here Comes the Sun" at the finale. I thought it sounded like everything Chekhov should be: sad-funny, funny-sad.

Chekhov continues to be thematic in my life. A year out of Yale, we did the first New York reading of my play *Uncommon Women and Others* upstairs at Playwrights Horizons very shortly after the theater had been transformed from its previous life as a burlesque house. I was beside myself when I found out that André Bishop, the artistic director of the young theater, and Laurie Heineman, an actress in my reading, both appeared in that legendary Harvard *Three Sisters.* There was only a slight problem, a slight cause for despair. My play, as most first drafts of first full-length plays often do, set out with gusto and had absolutely no ending. I had an idea about women and friend-ship and life goals—hopefully sad-funny, funny-sad—but still the play had no ending.

Finally, while looking around the room at André and Laurie and thinking about the *Three Sisters* at Harvard, I wondered what would happen to all of us and our comfortable artistic dreams, and I was reminded of the resonance of "We must go to Moscow." It was then, thinking about Chekhov, that I found the ending of my play.

The character Rita, at that point thirty and still a would-be novelist and probably the spirit of the play, puts her arm around her friends and says, "When we're forty, we'll be amazing." She had closed the first act, when she is twenty, by predicting. "When we're thirty, we're going to be pretty amazing." Time and age had become Rita's Moscow. Clearly, I was under the influence of a certain playwright, the Russian doctor.

I have no idea how many writers have finished a play, or understood where they were going, because they thought of Chekhov. I would tend to think their number is countless. Whereas in graduate school I related his plays to my own life, I now constantly think of his work as an arena, a goal for creating. There is no better reason to write than to attempt to barely touch where he succeeded.

Chekhov got to do it all. He was funny, he was sad. He was moving, he was satirical. *The Cherry Orchard,* a play about the demise of a family, a lifestyle, a class, is hilarious, yet painfully sad. In Chekhov, the comic and the tragic are not separated. They are melded into one spirit. For instance, Madame Ranevskaya in *The Cherry Orchard* weeps about Russia: "God can see I love my country, I love it warmly. I couldn't even see it from the train. I was crying the whole time." Then immediately through her tears she says, "All the same I must have my coffee."

As a writer, I wonder what kind of laugh she gets on "All the same I must have my coffee." It's not a big laugh—she doesn't pull out a rubber chicken—but it's exactly on target. From that one line, we know who she is, her pretensions, her pettiness, and she becomes recognizable, even likable. And the author remains nonjudgmental. He doesn't moralize. He doesn't call attention to himself. And he certainly doesn't make us laugh at Madame Ranevskaya. We just understand

her a little more. She's complicated and very human. The
humor Chekhov found in those complications is a humor I
constantly envy.

And Chekhov got to write big. His plays have large passes
of time. They open out from the verandas of an estate to take
in everyone, from the manservant to the landowner. In Act
Two of *Wild Honey,* as adapted by Michael Frayn, Platonov
emerges from the smoke of a train, stepping over the rail of a
track, and walks toward us. In our theater, tracks generally
appear in multimillion-dollar musicals on skates but hardly
ever in a play, a comedy, about the gentler foibles of the human
heart.

But it's not the bigness nor simply the comedy that I find so
impressive. I suppose it is the ability to be so keenly observant
and remain generous. Chekhov can see it all from everyone's
point of view, the aspiring of the new bourgeoisie, the pretensions and almost laziness of the landed gentry. He has the
overall vision of a changing society, and the individual insight
into each character. He doesn't reprimand his characters, he
just puts them out on the stage as honestly and with as much
craft as possible.

Ultimately, I think of his plays as the standard, because they
are so eminently theatrical. Chekhov tells us a story, makes us
laugh, makes us cry, changes a world, and it all happens before
us, live on stage. Madame Ranevskaya, Arkadina in *The Seagull,* and of course those three sisters are great parts because
they are not simply emblematic of an ideology, or a dramatic
device. They are impossible, arrogant, kind, smart, stupid,
funny, generous, self-absorbed, as only a great theater writer
could create them.

In anticipation of Peter Brook's staging of *The Cherry
Orchard,* I recently picked up a copy of the play. I was once
again struck by the subtitle—"A Comedy" in Three Acts.

How I wish we still had such a definition for comedy. Moreover, Lopakhin's plan to create summer cottages out of the cherry orchard seemed to almost uncannily parallel concerns regarding the remaining potato farms on Long Island's North Shore, or the future of Aspen as a ski resort. Chekhov wrote so well about his time and world that the piece is timeless.

I wish in some ways that the Hollywood agent had been onto something. I wish the playwright had been present for the actor's audition, and indeed had been in town for the Peter Brook production. I'd want to stop him and ask him how did he know? Just craft-wise, how did he know to have Madame Ranevskaya send for musicians and dance while they were selling her cherry orchard? And how did he know that her line about coffee could say so many things without explanation? Who was he thinking of when he first wrote, "I must go to Moscow"? Finally, how did he get it all to work at the same time and create something so honest, so truthful and profound? I'd want to ask him to teach me again and again and again. Which he does every time I see one of his plays.

"I terribly love anything called an estate in Russia. This word has not lost for me its poetic sound," Anton Chekhov wrote to his friend Nicolai Leikin on October 12, 1885. Seven years later, this grandson of a serf purchased with the money earned from his writing the ducal estate of Melihovo. One of its salient characteristics was its abundant crop of cherries.

In his final play, *The Cherry Orchard* (1904), Chekhov, who modestly believed himself to be merely the chronicler of his society, charted the passing of Russia's agrarian age. Caught in the morass of living under Czar Alexander III's autocracy, the orchard's fossilized, pathetically ineffectual owners spend the night dancing and playing billiards while their estate is being auctioned off in town. No one heeds the practical suggestions of the self-made man Lopakhin. His scheme to cut down the unproductive trees in order to parcel out the land into three-acre plots for dachas is rejected by the doomed, lovely Madame Ranevskaya: "Villas, summer visitors . . . it's so vulgar."

It is Lopakhin who will finally purchase "the pride of the whole province" in order to "save" it. The ironic twist lies in the fact that the new owner must destroy its beauty to make it economically viable. The play's tragic protagonist is the dismembered orchard, the perfect symbol of a vanishing order.

Lopakhin is a tool of an inexorable social process in which he is as trapped as are the aristocratic victims of the force of inertia. *The Cherry Orchard* is Chekhov's elegy to the Russia he loved, the testament of a dying artist.

How I Spent My Forties

My big sister Sandra and I were raised to be work-ing girls. This was somewhat surprising since our mother, Lola, was the Maimonides of feminine guile ideology. In fact, long before *The Rules* there was Lola's guide for the single gal. Among her most memorable nuggets remain: "Always look nice when you throw out the garbage— you never know who you might meet" and, my personal favorite, "A kiss or a spit, it's the same thing." It's important to understand that the latter was no slur on kisses. To the con-trary, since kisses are so delicious, would it kill you to give one to a frog who just might turn out to be a prince?

Unfortunately for my mother, her one rule of order that did resonate in both my sister's and my own life was from Lola's more spiritual canon. It was simply, "God helps those who help themselves." For us, daughters of the man who invented the annual Christmas classic, velveteen bows with bendable wire, girls who by the divine right of flocked goods could easily have been crowned Holy Brooklyn Princesses, this pithy bit of Lola's self-help translated into a lifetime agenda. All things being equal, we both preferred not to hang around the garbage in formal attire. We'd rather help ourselves.

In the late 1960s and 1970s Sandra became a marketing pioneer in an almost entirely male corporate America, breaking glass ceilings at General Foods and American Express. But when American Express merged with Shearson, Sandra was informed there would be no niche for her in the new configuration. She was too talented not to move forward and those few slots were obviously already taken. Unfortunately God seemed to give a little extra help to those who just happened to be male. At the same time, I brought her in for day surgery at NYU Hospital where a lump in her breast was diagnosed to be malignant. She was forty-five.

In addition to "Strazac"—very roughly, a general in the Polish army—Lola's other childhood name for Sandra was "Shtarker," a person who takes charge. Sandra approached both her health and any professional crisis with wartime-like strategy. On the one hand, since the cancer had not advanced to her lymph nodes, she systematically chose a lumpectomy, radiation, and dutiful checkups. She then reorganized her career as a headhunter at Russell Reynolds Associates, a slightly less stressful breather from corporate politics. Two years later, back at full speed, she became one of the twenty top executives at Citibank.

"I'm happier now than I've ever been in my life," she confided to me while walking on the beach just after she turned fifty-one. "Maybe it's because my daughters are so spectacular or my health, knock on wood, is good. For the first time in my life I really like being me. Do you know what I mean?"

I shook my head knowingly and falsely. Being thirteen years younger, I hadn't yet come to as comfortable a resting place.

At the time of our beach stroll my play *The Heidi Chronicles* was about to go into rehearsal. In the final scene Heidi at age thirty-eight adopts a baby alone. Whenever I was asked by interviewers if I believed a woman's happiness depended on having children, I'd always answer, "No, I am only responsible for my character. Heidi wants to have children."

What I never mentioned was that on the cusp of turning forty, I wanted to have children. And just like my big sister, I was convinced that God would help me help myself to beat the odds. It would just require some effort and organization.

After my play opened I made my first visit to the Mount Sinai Department of Reproductive Medicine. I sat across from a Dr. Hoffman, who assured me that I was completely in the ballpark. We just have to run a few tests, check my blood levels and uterine cavity.

Leaving the office at 101st Street and Fifth Avenue, I was skipping down the street. I was right. There was no such thing as "either/or." Women of my generation who postponed family life would not be punished. I would be living proof.

That spring ten years ago, *The Heidi Chronicles* won the Pulitzer Prize. My sister and I celebrated with friends and my brother, Bruce, at the Four Seasons restaurant, a place Sandra viewed as her personal cafeteria. As we toasted, I secretly vowed to take advantage of my professional good fortune and my sister's clean bill of health. I would concentrate now on having a child.

Dr. Hoffman called to inform me that I had a tendency to harvest uterine polyps. But it's no big problem, just a quickie day surgery.

"Sure. Absolutely." I was more than agreeable.

While coming to in the recovery room, a woman doctor with very thick glasses zeroed in on my recovery trolley.

"You're Wendy Wasserstein!" Her lenses fogged up at me. "You'll be glad to know that I saw your play and I found it so depressing I got married to a Jewish doctor right away."

"Mazel tov," I croaked at her.

I began studying fertility brochures and showed them to

the man I was currently involved with. For the first time I looked at him as a genetic pool. I'd say solid A minus: he looked like a faded Gary Cooper and was Phi Beta Kappa. I explained to him the glories of my FSH count and that with a little Clomid or Perganol I could be hatching eggs by the dozen.

A day after *The Heidi Chronicles* closed on Broadway, the phone rang in my L.A. hotel room. My gentleman caller had decided he'd rather we were just friends. Colette said, "No woman died of a broken heart over thirty." I vowed to show him. I'll lose forty pounds, write a new play, and then, of course, still have a baby. Time was never a significant issue to me.

I spent the next year avoiding fats, aerobically exercising, and writing *The Sisters Rosensweig*. Sandra lived in England in her early twenties and I dramatically transformed her into an American banker living in London in her mid-fifties. I decided to postpone the baby until there was a tangible father and the play was well on its feet.

The week *The Sisters Rosensweig* was first performed as a workshop at the Seattle Repertory Theater I received a call from my sister. After seven years in the clear, her persistent backache had been diagnosed as a recurrence of breast cancer. That night I sat in the audience of my play and watched as Pfeni, the youngest sister, a writer, sentimentally confessed to her banker sister Sara, "There is no one I rely on in life more than you. There is no one I am more grateful to than you."

I began to cry. But in an almost Pirandellian stroke my own character version of my sister cut off my self-indulgence.

"Pfeni, don't and I won't." Sara picks up a newspaper and refuses to cope with her sister's needy adoration.

When I returned to New York, Sandra and I made our first visit to Dr. James Speyer at NYU Hospital, Oncology. As soon

as they met, Sandra, backache and all, was suddenly trans-
ported to the James Madison High School math team and one-
upping the smartest boy in the class. It was her signature
mixture of flirtation and intellectual double jeopardy. Jim
graduated from Harvard in 1970, wore a watch with Native
American inlay, and grew up in a traditional Jewish house-
hold in Queens. If only my sister's visit had been as a board
of trustees consultant, she would have enjoyed the entire
encounter immensely.

Dr. Speyer prescribed tamoxifen and told her that, in retrospect, if only it had been around after her first diagnosis the
recurrence might well have been intercepted. I am to learn
that breast cancer treatment is a never-ending saga of "If only
we had had this when you had that, but you never know what's
coming next, so just hang in there."

An assistant came to the door. Apparently there'd been a
bomb threat ten blocks away at the United Nations. The
offices would be closing early.

First Avenue was bizarrely empty; no cars, no taxis, and a
smattering of pedestrians. Eerily it felt like we were drifting
through the eye of the storm, the inevitable sign of a post-
Soviet invasion.

Sandra and I got on the First Avenue bus. The passengers
were all eyeing each other as if we were in a heroic version of
It Happened One Night. I wanted to lead them in singing "Sit
down, you're rocking the boat!"

That night I slept at my sister's family-sized Madison Avenue apartment. Her beloved daughters were away at school. I
couldn't tell if my presence was an intrusion or a comfort.
I remained awake most of the night in my niece's bedroom. I
resolved to open *The Sisters Rosensweig* in New York for Sandra
and return to my quest of having a child.

At the opening-night party at Tavern on the Green my

sister Georgette was busy introducing herself as the real "Gorgeous," the Rosensweig sister so brilliantly portrayed by Madeline Kahn, while Sandra was happily giving seating instructions. The week before, she had had surgery, because she'd broken her arm putting on her panty hose. Clearly, the tamoxifen wasn't working.

When *The Sisters Rosensweig* moved from Lincoln Center to Broadway a few months later, Dr. Hoffman informed me that he too was changing residences, but in his case he was moving to Cleveland. He suggested I begin treatments with his colleague Dr. Michael Drews at Beth Israel immediately.

Inevitably some television executive will get an idea for the weekly hilarious and heartbreaking saga of a fertility doctor who in every episode brings us into the lives of couples, single women, gays and lesbians eager to conceive. For an upstanding, attractive prototype they should look no further than Dr. Michael Drews. Immediately he seemed like a friend one met years earlier at a first-rate liberal arts college; the biology major who wanted to talk late into the night about Anna Karenina, the premed student who married an actress.

In the theater we are trained to trust our instincts, and I decided immediately that this collaboration would work. With some hesitation I confided to my new physician that I was not involved with anyone at the moment, and he suggested a sperm catalogue from Wisconsin.

"Why Wisconsin?" I asked.

"I don't know. They eat cheese." He thought he was funny.

"Is that good for the sperm count?" I tried to ask nonchalantly.

"Depends on the cheese," he answered.

I received my first prescription of Clomid and felt I had finally joined the ovarian-stimulated generation.

I returned to Drews's office for what seemed to be a weekly

scrutiny of my eggs. Hotcha, I was producing three or four!
I bought a diary with visions of a publishable account of my
inseminations that would pay for baby's first Mozart play
group.

Our monthly rendezvous with sperm catalogue number
1147 was a nonhappening event. But I am resilient. I kept
getting my veins pricked for more FSH levels. I kept watching the sonogram machines for the amount of eggs I was
hatching. Dr. Drews suggested I move on to intermuscularly
injected Perganol, which would supposedly double the number of eggs.

"You know my sister has cancer." I looked up at him and
moved my legs under me.

"Yes, of course I know that." He tried to be sympathetic.

"So is this Perganol an insane thing to do?" I asked bluntly.

"We have no data that proves that," he answered me just as
bluntly.

"But eventually you will."

"You just need to have regular checkups." He reverted to
complete doctor mode.

I am terrified of needles and arranged to be shot up over
a counter at a Park Avenue drugstore called the Boghan
Pharmacy. Frankly, I was terrified of some cough-drop shop-
per hearing my name and asking me if I was writing anything new.

"Oh no!" I imagined myself being caught with my pants
down. "I'm just mooning Park Avenue."

Fertility treatments, far worse than any high school dance,
are a monthly confirmation of negative femininity. And it's
double the pleasure, double the fun because every disappoint-
ment is underscored by megadoses of hormones. There's nothing like sitting in a fertility doctor's office looking at the

photos of children they've nudged into creation and knowing you're the negative statistic. It becomes an addictive, undermining dream.

On Thanksgiving morning I walked down Central Park West toward my sister's annual family gathering. Lines of fathers with children sitting on their shoulders dotted the street for the Macy's parade. I began to get anxious. I was furious at myself, the women's movement, and the entire medical profession. I thought of Sandra valiantly going to work each day in her wigs and never mentioning her ongoing struggle. Comparatively, I felt spoiled and ridiculous. I was convinced that every photo of a baby in the doctor's office was a plot to negate my generation's sense of worth. Every fertility failure a reminder that for every door you've opened there'll be one slammed right in your face. I was now weeping uncontrollably. I couldn't tell if it was the endless injections, the disappointments, or the fear that any buoyant hopefulness I harbored was now completely dissipated.

I went home and hid before I saw Sandra and my family. I couldn't let them know this was happening to me.

Dr. Drews found another polyp and suggested this might be the cause of my monthly failures. Sandra, who now had pins in both her hips, insisted that she escort me to and from the surgery. As we sat in the waiting room I thought of us singing and dancing around my parents' living room to "S&W, Simply Wonderful Foods," a canned-foods theme song that conveniently used both our initials.

> *S&W, S&W, Simply Wonderful Foods*
> *We've got corn, tomatoes, onions, rice*
> *All the delicacies*
> *Look, look, whatever you need*

And the first female president of the card division would bellow in her baritone,

Look! We've even got birdseed!

Sandra delivered me home and I was violently ill from the anesthesia. My mother used to talk to us about girls who "good-*ga-davened*"—who in other words, davened or prayed right, who took care of themselves very-nicely-thank-you-very-much, who had doctor, lawyer, and real-estate-mogul husbands. My twice-divorced sister and I, on the other hand, took care of each other. As Lola said, we were 'smart but unteachable."

Sandra sat in my living room, her fingers unable to feel a hot teacup from a neuropathy she developed because of her latest chemotherapy. I, on the other hand, had brought my side effects on myself. I was learning things about sisterhood they never taught at Mount Holyoke Women's Studies.

Dr. Drews suggested that we move on to a live candidate. Since there was no permanent romance on the horizon, I asked an old and dear friend of mine to donate. He spent a happy morning at Park Avenue Fertility reading *Hustler*, *Penthouse*, and *The Life Story of Donny and Marie*. Although he was tested for every possible disease and dysfunction, his donation was frozen for six months for my safety.

After several more unsuccessful tries, Dr. Drews told me he was transferring to a new reproductive medicine group at St. Barnabas Hospital in Short Hills, New Jersey. Apparently he felt this was the far better option scientifically.

My friend and I made two trips to visit him in his new location. Although the shopping at the nearby mall was impressive, our results were not. My sister Sandra made me promise

I would take a rest from it all. I couldn't tell her that my fertility had become in my mind the parallel antidote to her cancer.

While I was at home that spring writing my new play, *An American Daughter,* Sandra called me crying.

"They've found cancer in my brain." She was gasping for breath. For the pride of the math team, an arm may be debatable but the brain was nonnegotiable.

"When do you next see my husband?" I asked softly, because she always laughed when I referred to Dr. Speyer as my spouse. "We have such a good marriage. I miss him. Can I come?"

"Sure, I know he misses you too." She was teary but giggled slightly. We both knew Jim Speyer was happily married.

While Sandra undressed for her examination Jim Speyer found me in the hallway. "I've never seen such a classic case of denial," he whispered. "I would be surprised if your sister was around in six months."

A year later my sister called me during a workshop of *An American Daughter* in Seattle to boast that her cancer markers were down and my husband was truly amazed at her progress. She'd mastered the details of every latest development in cancer treatment.

"I've stumped the star," she crowed to me. "I told him this new combination would work."

When I returned home from Seattle my gynecologist insisted I meet Dr. Maria Bustillo, who was the new director of Mount Sinai reproductive medicine. Maria was a feisty, bright woman who pulled no punches.

"We can try again with a process called GIFT or you can move on to a donor."

Adventures in fertility are not covered by insurance. I decided that before I spent thirteen thousand dollars on a high-tech procedure involving an anonymous donor egg, I'd investigate adoption.

I visited an international adoption agency. At the initial lecture we were informed that women over forty-five are only eligible for babies over three years old from Eastern European countries, and the same was true for babies from China. Also, because I was single and older, I was told that I must understand that I would be listed after any married or two-parent couples. The lecturer just wanted to be sure that I knew that my age and living situation made me less desirable. But it was nothing personal.

"Yes," I answered. "I understand."

"By the way, I admire your work," she added as she shook my hand.

Dr. Maria Bustillo performed a GIFT procedure on me at Mount Sinai. When the result was ultimately negative she reassured me that I had six leftover frozen egg and sperm combos in the Mount Sinai freezer.

"When you're up for it you can always try again!" She got up from the desk in her office and patted me on the shoulder.

I flew to Boca Raton, Florida, to meet Charlotte Danciu, a domestic adoption lawyer who had found glorious children for friends of mine. Charlotte was happy to help me adopt a child but she also had a surrogate mother she'd like me to meet. I asked her to please keep me informed about both.

An American Daughter opened on Broadway to decidedly mixed notices. The play about a woman's failed surgeon general nomination was criticized for being about too many things.

"Women's lives are always about too many things. But it's very hard to say anything about women now," my big sister tried to reassure me. "It's much easier for everyone to believe we're past it."

Two days after my opening my sister and I flew to Paris for my brother Bruce's wedding party. Sandra was decidedly frail and limping. Her daughters held her arm as she attempted to walk down the stairs. For convenience' sake my brother had moved the Passover seder a day early so my family and Sandra could celebrate it together. It's a feat that's right up there with parting the Red Sea.

"Why is this night different from all other nights?" my nephew asked the first question at lunch in a private tapestry-laden dining room at the Ritz Hotel.

Sandra immediately rolled her eyes at me. I smirked at her and silently wondered what I'd do if she wasn't at the table.

I arranged to meet Charlotte's surrogate mother, whom I'll call Nancy, at a coffeehouse in Seattle. She's a terrific woman; a mother of four and a champion of reproductive rights. I asked her why she wants to do this for me.

"I like the idea of helping you, and I could use the money," she admitted frankly.

We talk about Alaska and the favorable percentage of men to women.

"Oh yeah, I could find you someone right away!" Nancy assured me.

Nancy undercut her seriousness with an obvious sense of humor. There was something deeply human about Nancy and my connection. I voted for surrogacy.

I arranged for Nancy to fly to Florida for the insemination. Since her daughter lived there she would also be able to work in a family visit. But just as I was preparing to fly down for Nancy's in vitro procedure, I received a call from the Florida doctor.

"Your eggs are scrambled. They were not properly packed or frozen. We cannot proceed." His tone was matter-of-fact.

Nancy went home to Alaska. I was convinced that I'd discovered a truth even Lola in all her wisdom hadn't uncovered. Except perhaps for the magically good-*ga-davened*, there are still specific women's issues. They have not all been resolved, rather, they are simply unspoken. Women may be "jugglers," but the balancing act isn't always between making time for tumbling tots' classes, manicures, and professional fulfillment.

Over the summer I continued to correspond with Nancy and she offered to use her own eggs with the donor of my choice. I was stunned by her generosity.

Our next try I was able to fly to Florida to be with her. The night of Nancy's procedure we spent hours in the Boca Raton Resort and Club with her daughter and Charlotte Danciu, applying tattoos to our nails and mud packs to our faces.

I was in Chicago when I heard that the outcome was negative. Nancy seemed deeply disappointed. I went to the Water Tower Movie Theater and devoured a bag of chocolate licorice, Sandra's favorite candy.

That August Sandra requested to celebrate her sixtieth birthday in London. We met for drinks in the Savoy Lounge— Sandra, her best friend from her London days, Edwina, and an English rheumatologist friend of mine, Dr. Rodney Hughes. I gave my sister a watercolor by Dorothy Hepworth of a woman reading. During her illness Sandra had become obsessed with her "great books" reading group. A simple call to say how are you seemed to always digress into a half-hour discourse on St. Augustine.

Sandra held up the painting as I explained to her that the artist was the English painter Stanley Spencer's wife's lesbian lover.

"Yes, I know," she curtly cut off the conversation. I somehow doubt that she did, but Sandra even in her very frail state was a master of authority. My sister, however, was displaying troubling spasms of overt sentimentality. We ordered another glass of champagne and she lifted her glass to toast us.

"I can't tell you how lucky I feel at this moment," her voice began to crack. "I have the best possible family and friends. This has been a great birthday."

I knew then we were very near the end.

I arranged the next night for Sandra to get tickets to David Hare's play *Amy's View*. Having already seen the play, I thought the elements of the evening would be tailor-made for Sandra: Dame Judi Dench, mother-daughter conflict, successful actress, financial crisis, the demise of the class system—in other words, everything a successful Anglophile career woman and single mother could want.

The following morning she left me a note before she took off with Edwina for a holiday.

"I saw the most extraordinary play last night called *Amy's View*. I can't wait to discuss it with you. You really should go out of your way to see it."

As I threw that note away I wondered if the painkillers had blurred her memory or if the disease had reappeared in her brain. Of course it's possible that both she and Dr. Speyer had decided not to mention it to me. He had long ago stopped making predictions.

Early in October I was back in rehearsal for an evening of one-acts inspired by Shakespeare sonnets for the Acting Company. As I was dressing to leave my house Sandra called to say she'd been having terrible pains in her stomach.

"Maybe you'd like to pay a quick visit with me to your husband?" she asked.

She picked me up in front of my house with her car service and we made the familiar trek downtown. My sister was amazingly thin. She had lost her appetite and was half delighted that her weight was below average.

When we entered the hospital lobby Sandra grabbed onto a desk. She didn't have the strength to get to the elevator. She stopped to rest as I found a wheelchair.

Dr. Speyer examined Sandra while I sat in his office staring at the East River. When I was two years old my big sister dressed me in my brother's blue jeans and wheeled me to James Madison High School to show me off to her friends. We are New York girls: Brooklyn-born, raised on the Upper East Side. My sister and I are the local talent.

I felt a hand on my back.

"I believe your sister's cancer has advanced to her liver." Dr. Speyer looked honestly distracted. "It's your sister so I can't predict anything exactly, but I think we are nearing the end of a long journey."

I decided not to bother with rehearsals and took a ride with Sandra back uptown.

"I've worked out a plan with your husband," Sandra said with her efficient clip as we drove past Grand Central. "We will try one more round of chemotherapy, and if that doesn't work Speyer will make the arrangements for something at home with the girls."

We were back in logistics mode. The sentimentality was now completely absent. She could have been arranging a new Chinese market for the gold card. She never mentioned how frightened she must have been. That would have been too humiliating. And if a kiss and a spit are the same thing, then a humiliation was lurking behind any intimate corner.

The week before Christmas a Broadway producer who had asked me to write a stage version of *Swing Time* sent me videos of every Fred Astaire movie ever made. Sandra, for the first

time excluding her hospital stays for broken limbs and
chemotherapies, had taken a week off from her work. Or rather
she had chosen to work from home. To explain my constant
visits, I told her I had an assignment to watch all these films
and I needed her to help me.

Sandra insisted that both her daughters go out of town for
Christmas. She didn't want her illness to impinge on their
holiday. Her daughter Samantha had taken a semester off
from UC Berkeley Graduate School to be with her. But Sandra
was adamant that this would be a particularly good time for
Samantha to drive cross-country.

Every afternoon we would watch a musical extravaganza
like *Ziegfeld Girl* or *Roberta.* I brought over a cassette of *The
Object of My Affection,* a film I wrote that had just been completed. Sandra, with great difficulty, moved from her bed to
the chaise lounge by the television to watch it. I couldn't help
but notice her trying so hard to concentrate, moving her body
in obvious pain to find more comfortable positions.

"I liked the old man. He was funny!" she said at the end of
the movie. "Who was that?"

"Nigel Hawthorne." I made no mention that it was almost
unbearable to me that my sister the Anglophile didn't recognize him.

I wanted to ask her what else she thought, not just about
the movie but about everything: marriage, children, diet soda,
our parents. I wanted a lifetime's worth of advice.

"Sandra's calcium levels are high and Dr. Speyer wants her
in the hospital tonight," Betsy Carter, a family friend, called
me bright and early Christmas Eve morning.

When I arrived at Sandra's apartment her daughter Jenifer
was packing her up for a brief hospital stay. Jenifer was scheduled, as per Sandra's wishes, to fly to Aspen that night. Betsy
Carter snapped on Sandra's bra and pulled her sweater over her

head. Jenifer offered to take Sandra down to NYU before the enforced departure.

Coincidentally, Dr. Speyer was also scheduled to leave. Sandra claimed it was no problem since he had come to visit her at home the other night. Even in her excruciating state she managed to twinkle slightly with the triumph of a home visit. She had explained her entire prognosis to him.

That Christmas Eve I watched *Damsel in Distress,* a Fred Astaire mystery spoof, with my sister at NYU Hospital. She made me promise again and again that I would not tell the ending of the film to her friend Joanne or our former sister-in-law Chris when they visited the following day. My sister wanted the volume louder and began pushing buttons on her cellular phone.

"There, that's better." She looked at me triumphantly.

"Yes." I avoided her face, trying not to broadcast my concern.

"You should sit up straight," she suddenly ordered me. "You know in this light you're very pretty."

I sloughed it off.

"No, you should go look at yourself in the mirror. You're very pretty."

Then I did exactly what I was told like a good baby sister. But as I looked in the mirror I saw Sandra yawning. I kissed her good night. "I'll come back a little later."

When I came back later that night Sandra Meyer had already gone into a coma.

My family held a twenty-four-hour vigil around her bed. Sandra, who could become more than a little irritated by a misplaced coffee mug, would have had a fit at the paper cups and sandwich wrappers in her room. She was, however, consistent in what she could control. Throughout her final hospital stay, Sandra's hands were perfectly manicured and her face youthfully dewy from years of Estée Lauder antiaging creams. Looking at her made me wish that Estée had perfected creams that were equally effective in addressing my sister's far more pressing needs.

On the fourth night of our vigil, Sandra's daughters and I decided to give her some privacy. After all, she was a woman who coveted her solitude. I was in a taxi driving over the Brooklyn Bridge into Manhattan when she died. Sandra, who was so concerned with showing our family a world outside our comfortable childhood one in Flatbush, would have appreciated that. She died alone, without the hand-holding and tears of a television movie. If she wasn't setting the rules, no one else would be either. Sandra was the ultimate big sister.

My family scattered her ashes on a beach in East Hampton on New Year's Eve, 1997. Sandra died at sixty.

Almost a year after my sister's death, I was having lunch at the Café des Artistes with a friend when an attractive man I didn't recognize tapped me on the shoulder.

"Wendy, it's me, Michael Drews." I looked up and immediately remembered my most compassionate fertility doctor. "How've you been?"

"I'm fine," I smiled up at him from my gravlax. "I'm OK and I've given up on that other thing." I couldn't believe I was referring to children as "that other thing," but I really didn't want to go to that place again.

"That's why I came over." His voice was still cheerful. "Things have improved dramatically since you started and I'd say you've got a very good chance for success today. Call me. I think we can get this right now."

"No, really. I've given up on that." I made the sign of the cross like I was warding off a vampire.

The week before Christmas I got a call from Jim Speyer. He wanted to meet me for drinks at the Harvard Club.

"Your sister beat so many odds by the end, I let her call the shots," he told me over a straight scotch. "She wanted that final chemotherapy and my feeling was, it was her disease. Who was I to say no? The only reason I'm sorry I wasn't there at the end was I might have made it easier for her daughters."

"I just want to know how you are able to do your job," I asked him.

"How else would I get to know people like Sandra?" he answered quite quickly.

"But you get to know them at the end of their life—"

"Look at your sister," he interrupted me. "That was a remarkable time in her life. It's amazing she lasted as long as she did. Everything was breaking down. I will never forget her."

Sandra would have been thrilled. He had been her husband, not mine, all along.

I still believe women's lives are about too many things. But sometimes there is clearly a convergence. I think of lifting Sandra up into a London taxi for her sixtieth birthday. She would always try to the best of her ability. I, on the other hand, ever since my big sister's death, was becoming a cynic. I had come to believe not only that God didn't help those who helped themselves, but also that he couldn't care less.

When I called Michael Drews and told him I was willing to try once more, it was Sandra's obstinate and heroic determination that made me do it. Just as she had guided most of the more ambitious efforts of my life, I was neither particularly brave nor insane. I was just, one more time, emulating my big sister.

Days of Awe:
The Birth of Lucy Jane

got up at 5:00 a.m. on August 27 to write Fay Francis's eulogy. A descendant of New York's Harriman family, Fay lived on the Upper East Side and was always properly decked out in her pumps, gloves, and Schlumberger brooches. For the past two decades, I had eaten Christmas lunch at the Colony Club with Fay and her son André Bishop, who is the artistic director of the Lincoln Center Theater and one of my oldest friends. Every year at cocktail time Fay would present me with a purse suitable for the Queen Mother. And every year just before the plum pudding arrived, Fay's escort, Roland Peas, would introduce me to General MacArthur's widow.

As I began to gather my memories of Fay that morning, I felt a tingling from my left elbow to my hand. I figured it had to be psychosomatic. I had never been asked to be the opening act at an Episcopalian service before. Furthermore, although Fay was eighty-four, her death had unnerved me. I remembered my last conversation with her. Because she had been ill the previous Christmas, we had canceled our lunch, but I had called to wish her well.

"Thing is, lamb, I worry about you," she had said in her stately old New York accent. "All the men your age are either married or gay, and the single ones want young things. You have your work and your friends, but you deserve some personal happiness, too."

For the funeral, I put on my most Fay-like gray suit with my most Fay-like gray pearls. I even made an appointment at an Upper East Side salon to get my hair blown straight. If I was going to give a eulogy at St. James Church, I was going to look like St. James Church. And anyway, I was planning to leave for England that night for a week's vacation, and as my mother, Lola, always said, "It wouldn't kill you to look nice." Unfortunately, instead of making my hair shiny and sleek, the hairdresser decided to express herself through my natural curls. I arrived at the church looking like an extra from *Yentl*.

André's brother George, an Oxford-educated priest, presided over the service.

Wearing a white satin gown with gold vestments, George told us that he knew his mother had found redemption at the end of her life because in April she had sent pears to his father's new wife, and in May, Georgia peaches. I had never known that the Fruit of the Month Club was the road to salvation.

When I finally reached the pulpit and began to speak, my voice cracked.

Maybe it was my affection for Fay, or the unaccustomed tingling in my hand. Or maybe I was simply unhinged by the passing of time. Looking out into the pews of the church, I recognized theater colleagues whom I had known for a quarter of a century. James Lapine, the director of *Sunday in the Park with George,* was whispering to William Finn, the composer and lyricist of *Falsettoes.* Gerald Gutierrez, the director of *The*

Heiress, was staring hard at me as a reminder to pause before I told my Queen Mother jokes. We had all become, over the years, each other's continuing history and family.

Of course, as with most families, those members of mine who had gathered at St. James that morning didn't have the slightest idea what was going on in my life. On August 17, 1999, I was forty-eight years old and six months pregnant.

It wasn't like I got knocked up. Most forty-eight-year-old women don't.

The previous March, I was lying on a day-surgery gurney in Short Hills, New Jersey, watching my egg and sperm combination platter on live-action video. An embryologist in the room next door was siphoning the embryos, which resembled water droplets, from a petri dish into a tiny tube. It was a surreal cross between PBS *Nature* and the Food Channel.

"You see your signature in the dish?" Michael Drews, my longtime fertility doctor, asked me as he watched the video with me in his hospital scrubs.

I nodded.

"That way you know for sure it's yours," he explained.

"Would you excuse me for a moment?" he asked, and went into the lab next door.

My mind wandered to my best friend Susan in the eighth grade and how we'd spend endless hours talking about sex and falling in love. Thirty-odd years later, I thought, I'm lying here conceiving a child with *Emeril Live.*

Dr. Drews returned with the magic tube, which was the width of a pipe cleaner.

As he inserted it into my uterus, he said, "Wendy, are you still writing?"

"Yes. I started a new play," I said. "But it's not as interesting as this!"

When the procedure was finished he shook my hand and wished me luck.

"Let's keep our fingers crossed," he said when the procedure was over. As he left, I noticed that he was wearing clogs. Many health-care professionals do.

The following night I got on a flight to Europe. Looking out at the stars, I began to weep. I wasn't exactly crying for fear that this last effort would again prove to be futile. For eight years I had believed that the greatest regret of my life would be that I was childless. I realized now that I was finally willing to give that up. In the past decade I had lost my sister and most likely the possibility of bearing children. That night I was perfectly content to be uprooted, in space, alone.

Two weeks later, after I returned from my trip, there was a message on my answering machine from a lab in New York: "Congratulations. You're pregnant." My due date was approximately Christmas, 1999. It was a millennium prophecy close to a miracle.

After Fay Francis's funeral, I shared a taxi from St. James Church with James Lapine and Bill Finn.

"Could you believe the thing about the fruit?" Bill laughed.

"Are you really going to England tonight?" James asked me.

"I think so. I just have to go to a doctor's appointment first."

"What doctor?" Bill immediately jumped on me. "You never go to doctors."

"Oh, you know," I replied. "Just routine checkup stuff."

My decision to keep my pregnancy a secret from most of my friends was a simple one. I knew that I was teetering on the high end of high risk. If the baby didn't come to term after all these years of trying, I wanted it to be a matter of personal loss and not a public one. My plan was to wait until Labor Day, well into my seventh month, and then inform my friends that the twenty pounds I had recently gained were not the result of bad habits and anxiety. And Labor Day was when my brother, Bruce, and his wife were expecting their second child.

"Let me take your blood pressure." A nurse wrapped a familiar Velcro-lined cuff around my upper arm. The drill at the Eastside Women's OB/GYN Associates was always the same: urine sample, weight, blood pressure, followed by a visit with the attending doctor.

The nurse looked at me sternly. "Your blood pressure is a little high," she said. "Relax for a few minutes. Don't be nervous. I'll be back."

Although I'm a big, healthy, hearty girl, even in routine circumstances I could be voted Miss White Coat Syndrome. Ever since my sister's death I've been convinced that any protracted time spent with a health care professional is a prelude to surprise terminal illness.

The nurse returned in five minutes and wrapped the cuff around my arm again.

"It's higher now!" She seemed to be slightly irritated with me. "I told you to relax! Lie on your left side and the doctor will be with you in a few minutes."

I reached for a magazine and came upon a detailed account of Cindy Crawford's successful pregnancy: Cindy is "over the moon" about her baby. Cindy does yoga and is working out all the way through. Cindy never has swollen fingers and legs. Cindy never had to lie on her left side.

Twenty minutes later Dr. Laurie Goldstein came into the room. She still wears the insignia of her activist generation: dangling earrings, little makeup, and evolved-graduate-student attire. Dr. Goldstein is deeply committed to women's health issues.

"I hear your blood pressure is high," she said, wrapping the Velcro cuff around me again.

"Well, I get nervous. And I was planning on leaving for London tonight." I was rambling anxiously, eager to be on my way.

"Did you know you have protein in your urine?" she asked me.

"Not really. I spoke at a funeral this morning."

"Try to relax." She started squeezing the blood pressure pump again.

I held up Cindy's pregnancy photos. "You shouldn't keep things like this around your office."

"You're absolutely right." She looked me in the eye. "I want you to get into a taxi and go over to Mount Sinai Hospital. Your blood pressure is very high and there's a chance you have preeclampsia."

"Who?" I asked her in a panic.

She explained, "Preeclampsia is a high blood pressure condition which can lead to liver and kidney failure. I'm not saying that you have it. And if you do, most likely we can treat it by keeping you in bed until your delivery."

"I'm sorry," I said. When I'm frightened, I become excessively polite. "Can I go home first to get a few things?"

"Get a friend to bring them to you. I want you to go right now."

Half an hour later my gray St. James suit was strewn over a stool in the labor and delivery ward.

Michele K. Silverstein, a doctor in her thirties with brown curly hair and kind brown eyes behind wire-rimmed glasses, is the junior member of the Eastside Obstetrics Group. She is also what every modern Jewish mother secretly hopes her daughter will turn out to be. Michele has the earnestness of a science jock, but it's offset by a skating-rink-sized diamond from her hematologist husband.

"Are you comfortable in here?" she asked about my quarters.

"I'm in a Kafka story, Michele!"

"Look, I hope it's just for the night," she said. "We'll monitor you and probably send you home tomorrow." For all her youthfulness, Dr. Silverstein has an authoritative directness. "I'll see you later. I've got a delivery next door."

I called William Ivey Long, an old friend from the Yale Drama School who had been my fertility confidant for many years. He was in the middle of designing costumes for the upcoming musicals *Contact* and *Swing* and for the Broadway play *Epic Proportions*. Even so, he rushed over to spend the night on the reclining guest chair in my hospital room.

Hospitals are places where no one sleeps. Bells ring throughout the night and every room has a twenty-four-hour open-door policy. Every two hours I was awakened to have my blood pressure taken. By now I was able to recognize the approach of the dreaded blood pressure machine by the creaking of tiny wheels along the hospital corridor. At four in the morning a nurse told me, "It's 189 over 100. Relax and lie on your left side."

As far as I can make out, relaxing and lying on your left side is the treatment for preeclampsia. Preeclampsia, I came to learn, is better known by its longtime name, toxemia. It is most often associated with protein in the patient's urine, swelling of extremities, and hypertension. In a pregnant woman, the condition can lead to liver and kidney failure or to a coma-inducing brain seizure. An affected fetus can suffer from stunted growth or, in the worst cases, can die as a result of the placenta being separated from the uterus. The one certain cure for preeclampsia is delivery. Therefore, when the condition occurs during the third trimester, mothers are immediately scheduled for childbirth.

Laurie Goldstein reappeared the next morning with the bad news: I showed all the classic signs of preeclampsia. I was to be moved to the fourth floor for a weekend of observation. I tried to take deep breaths and think about those pears from the Fruit of the Month Club. Maybe they could be my salvation, too.

I had never been hospitalized before, and hadn't realized the experience was a nonstop meet-and-greet. In addition to my bihourly blood pressure monitoring, I was suddenly being treated by rotating cardiologists. One of them, Robert Phillips, an M.D./Ph.D. cardiologist, came into my room on Sunday. He seemed accessible, and with the right anecdote, I could make him giggle.

On Monday, after taking my pressure three times, Dr. Phillips explained the various blood pressure medications I was taking. The phenobarbital, he told me, could make me groggy and forgetful. Then he mentioned that another doctor would be covering for him the following week because he had to go to Houston. I asked him why.

"I'm going to the National Space Biomedical Research Institute," he told me. "There's going to be a human settlement on Mars, and I want to be part of Mount Sinai's advisory team."

"Mars! Really?" I was sure I must be experiencing a phenobarbital reaction.

"I'm competing against doctors from Stanford and Penn," he told me, delighted that I was interested.

"You know, it's important you get this," I said. "They're always sending people like John Glenn or Sally Ride into space. They need Jews from Mount Sinai!"

"Try to lie on your left side," he gently admonished me.

I rolled over. "Listen, you've got the old *ma nishtanah* problem here. Why is your proposal for Mars different than anybody else's? You probably need to punch it up."

"Punch it up?" he asked.

"Yeah, sure. You need a laugh on the third line," I advised him. "Like a family anecdote, they always warm the room."

"That's good," Dr. Phillips said, impressed, and he handed me a copy of his proposal: "The Effect of Microgravity on Cardiac Hemodynamic."

Monday morning as I was trying to decipher Dr. Phillips's cardiovascular-speak, Rebecca Brightman, the final member of my troika of female obstetricians, appeared with Laurie and Michele. Rebecca Brightman is a beauty. With her black hair and bright blue eyes, she reminds me of Suzanne Pleshette in her pre–Bob Newhart phase.

My doctors wanted me to stay in the hospital until as close to my due date as possible. Since I was twenty-five weeks pregnant, that meant three months at Mount Sinai, far longer than it took Moses to get his tablets.

The next day, while I was calculating how I would inform the Princeton theater department that I would not be teaching playwriting that fall, Dr. Richard Berkowitz, the hospital's head of obstetrics, came in. In his opinion, my preeclampsia was potentially life-threatening and I should prepare myself to have the baby that afternoon, depending on lab results.

As I was absorbing my revamped schedule, a nurse came in and told me to clean up my room because I was expected to be out of there by 11:00 a.m.

For the first time I didn't care about being voted Miss Mount Sinai Congeniality. I lowered my voice. "You know, it's impossible to lie on my left side and to be out of this room at eleven a.m. I'm a person, not a grouper!"

I had no idea where the grouper came from. Maybe it was Christian imagery left over from the mass at St. James. Or maybe I was starring in a pro-life Christian docudrama warning young girls not to grow up into self-centered heathens like me: Marry young and procreate!

Two hours later, I was prepped for surgery and lying on a gurney awaiting a cesarean. I was placed in a wait station separated only by curtains from other about-to-be-delivered mothers. Michele K. Silverstein came in to see me.

"You all right?" she asked.

"Fine."

"I've asked Ian Holtzman, who runs the neonatal unit here, to talk to you about premature babies."

In all my years of seeking after fertility, the possibility of having a premature child had never occurred to me. The trick had been to get pregnant. Period.

Dr. Ian Holtzman is a warm, energetic man in his fifties with a gray beard. When he came to see me in the wait station, he said, "You should know that babies born after only twenty-five weeks' gestation are at a higher risk for having lung or brain damage than those born even at thirty weeks. That's not to say it's inevitable." He smiled at me with an ingratiating familiarity. "But you should know."

I thanked him before he disappeared behind the curtain. Lying on my gurney, I decided that I'd moved on from Christian docudrama to the plague portion of the Passover seder, when we dip our pinkies repeatedly into wine to represent the hideous disasters the good Lord inflicted on the Egyptians: locusts, frogs, pestilence, infertility, preeclampsia, brain damage.

A nurse stuck her head in: "Your ex-husband is here!" I had no idea who she could be talking about.

My friend Gerry Gutierrez pulled back the curtain. "Hello, darling," he said. "I heard you're not a grouper!"

Suddenly, Michele K. Silverstein burst in. "So, we're not operating," she said.

"I'm her ex-husband," Gerry introduced himself.

Dr. Berkowitz joined us in my curtain closet. "I just spoke to the world expert in Tennessee on preeclampsia," he told us. "He says in cases as severe and early in a pregnancy as yours, every day in the womb is equal to three days in the NICU [the popular acronym for neonatal intensive care unit]. The longer we can keep that baby inside of you without damaging your health, the better the baby's chances for survival are." He smiled at me broadly. "So I've gotten you a room back on the labor and delivery floor and we'll just keep you there as long as we can."

My ex-husband pushed the gurney down the hall. I looked up at him and said, "Now we've got time to punch up a speech for this guy who wants to go to Mars."

There's a spherical Pomadaro sculpture in the Arthur Ross Courtyard at Mount Sinai that resembles a similar work at the Vatican. Patients on the labor and delivery floor like to concentrate on it in between Lamaze breaths. Most look at it for a few hours or, at most, a night. I settled in to stare at it from Labor Day until Christmas.

When I called my friend Jane Rosenthal to tell her about my new fall plans, she immediately swung into action. Jane is a movie producer and a crackerjack organizer. She reached William Ivey Long during the final dress rehearsal of *Contact,* and told him to get up to Mount Sinai to redecorate my room.

At nine in the morning, William arrived with an armful of coordinated blue floral curtains, pillows, and Monet posters. The room, formerly a beige netherworld, became the decorator showroom of the second floor. Nurses and hospital attendants popped in throughout the day to ask William for color and contouring tips.

Every day at Mount Sinai was the same.

6:00 a.m.   Weigh in, blood pressure, blood test.

7:00 a.m.   Residents rounds led by Dr. Berkowitz.

10:00 a.m. Becky Brightman or Michele K. Silverstein comes by to tell me the results of my blood test and whether I could expect to put off having the baby another day.

11:00 a.m. Sonogram.

12:00 p.m. Lunch.

The afternoons melted into naps interrupted by blood pressure monitoring or a half hour of fetal heart rate monitoring.

The nights were slightly more challenging. To ward off any chance of seizure, I was now attached to an intravenous magnesium drip, which made me extremely nauseous. I've never been good at asking for help. As an Ethical Culture School graduate, I have always believed that my purpose is to be generous and to serve others. But when I was too ill to make it to the bathroom, Angela, the African-American night nurse, who wore a medallion that said "Girl Power" around her neck, would bring me a pan for the nausea. She gave me soothing sponge baths, too. I quickly became obsessed with the disparity between Angela's salary and Demi Moore's.

The only time I left my stylish nest in labor and delivery was to have a daily sonogram with Dr. Joanne Stone and Dr. Keith Eddleman, the coauthors of *Pregnancy for Dummies*.

"Do you want to know the sex of the baby?" Dr. Stone asked me one morning. Joanne Stone, like Becky Brightman, is one of the new glamour breed of women doctors. She is a svelte mother of two who wears miniskirts and high-heeled pumps while searching for fetal heartbeats.

Before the preeclampsia, I had decided to let the baby's sex be a surprise. But now I wanted all my cards on the table.

"It's a girl." Dr. Stone showed me the outline of my baby's gender. There's her hand, she said, moving her ultrasound mouse over my goo-covered stomach.

I looked up at the screen and saw a tiny hand waving at me as if to say, "Hold on, Mom, I'm coming!"

"Do you want a copy of that?" Dr. Stone asked me.

I kept it by my bedside for the rest of my stay.

When I made it a full week without my kidneys collapsing, my doctors were thrilled with me. My anxiety level, however, was mounting for a different reason. I was developing an obsessive fear about my mother. I had told her a week earlier about my pregnancy, but she had no idea that I was in the hospital.

The last time my mother had been in a hospital, she had watched her oldest daughter die of cancer. I knew it would be impossible for me to lie on my left side and to keep my blood pressure down with my mother sitting by, weeping, and seeing Sandra in me. So for her sake, and for the sake of my daughter, I decided I could not invite my mother to labor and delivery.

"Your mother called me, crying," my agent told me just after Labor Day. "She asked me where you were."

My blood pressure was up again. I left a message on my mother's machine: "Hello, Mother. I'm still in England with Flora. I'm having a wonderful time."

It is almost impossible to draw blood from my veins even in the best of circumstances. After twelve days in the hospital, my arms had the multiple track marks of a heroin addict. Also, the news about my condition was suddenly not so good.

"Your blood platelets are beginning to drop," Becky Brightman informed me at 10:00 a.m. one day. "Don't panic. It's a matter of the entire picture."

But I was panicking, and not just about my platelets. A nurse had just told me that my brother Bruce and his pregnant wife, Claude, had booked the delivery room across the hall from me for the following week. I started imagining a scene from a Marx Brothers movie, *A Day at the Hospital:* while Bruce is telling his wife to breathe deeply, he sees me being wheeled out to the sonogram room with my magnesium-drip sidekick.

On Sunday morning, sixteen days after I was admitted, Michele K. Silverstein came to see me.

"How would you like to have a baby today?" she asked me.

"Am I having a baby today?" I squinted at her.

"I think so."

"Can I make a few calls?" I asked.

"Sure. Let's say one o'clock. Becky's driving in. We'll deliver you together."

I called my brother. My entire family was gathered at his apartment that morning to celebrate his anniversary.

"Bruce, don't say anything," I whispered. "I'm at Mount Sinai. I'm having a baby today."

"I'll be right there," he said, and hung up.

At 12:45 I was wheeled into the operating room accompanied by my two women obstetricians, two women nurses, a female anesthesiologist, and Gerald Gutierrez. I felt as if I were back in class at Mount Holyoke in 1967, with one visiting male student from Amherst. It was familiar in the best possible way.

I don't think I really connected lying on that brightly lit

table with bringing new life into the world. Looking down at Becky and Michele with their intelligent professional faces and perfectly coiffed heads, I imagined they were having a heated conversation in the Neiman Marcus shoe department.

"J. P. Tods." Becky examines my pelvis.

"Manolo Blahnik." Michele passes Becky an instrument.

"Wendy, can you feel this?" Becky tapped my stomach after the epidural started.

"Yes." I could feel pricks on my flesh.

My cesarean lasted approximately one hour. Gerry held my head. At 2:25 I heard a cry and saw a baby out of the corner of my eye.

"Congratulations. You have a daughter," Becky Brightman said to me.

The baby was immediately whisked away to the hospital's neonatal intensive care unit on the fifth floor. She weighed 790 grams, or roughly one pound twelve ounces.

Premature babies, much like the plot of an Oscar Wilde play or a Gilbert and Sullivan opera, have two birthdays. The first one, which is on the birth certificate, is the moment the baby hits the labor and delivery room running. The second one, which is based on the anticipated delivery date, is the "corrected age." For instance, a child born two months early would five months later have a birth certificate age of five months, but only three months old corrected. Development for the first two years of life is based on corrected age, not legal age. The babies in the NICU are, in corrected age, the youngest people on the earth: minus and still counting.

That night André Bishop and my brother came to visit me. Slipping in and out of consciousness, I told Bruce I was going to name my daughter Brooklyn in honor of the borough where we were raised. He looked at me as if I'd said I was going to call her Bensonhurst or Navy Yard. I asked Bruce to go upstairs to visit the baby because I wouldn't be able to move until tomorrow. André stayed with me.

"You can't call your daughter Brooklyn," André said in his deep authoritative voice.

"That Spice Girl did."

"You're not a Spice Girl," he pointed out.

Because Gerald Gutierrez was in the delivery room with me, he was given a plastic hospital bracelet that said "father." This allowed him unlimited access to the intensive care unit. All visitors without wristbands are justifiably limited.

At 9:00 p.m. my brother Bruce approached the desk at the NICU with my friend Peter Schweitzer, a CBS News producer, and announced, "I'm here to see Baby Wasserstein."

"Do you have some ID?" the receptionist asked.

"I'm Bruce Wasserstein," my brother answered. "I'm the baby's father."

"Someone else came in earlier that said he was the father," she said suspiciously.

"Yes. That's right. Well, he's the father, and I'm the father"— Bruce then grabbed Peter—"and he's the father, too!"

In short order, my brother, an iconoclastic investment banker who had protected oil companies from T. Boone Pickens and advises movie studios about the dot-com world, managed to secure from the receptionist permanent visitation rights as a parent.

By the next day, the news that I had had a baby flashed through the theater community. One rumor that would become a particular favorite of mine was that I had been pregnant and hadn't known it.

The morning after I delivered, Dr. Berkowitz came in to tell me that I was still doing great. My blood pressure was down and my platelets were heading back toward normal. The news about my daughter was not as good. Ian Holtzman and his neonatal residents came in to see me at 8:00 a.m.

"Your daughter had a bad night," he informed me. "You've got a very sick little girl, I just want you to know that." He smiled kindly and left.

This was the first I had heard of my daughter's condition. I couldn't really take it all in. My pediatrician explained that the illness was hyaline membrane disease, a lung affliction common in premature babies. I knew that it had caused the death of Jacqueline Kennedy's third child, Patrick.

After dinner, a nurse wheeled me upstairs to see my baby for the first time. My family genes do not specialize in shoulder blades or collarbones. The first thing I noticed about my daughter was that she has shoulders like Audrey Hepburn when she wears that white strapless Cecil Beaton number in the film version of *My Fair Lady*. Even in her Isolette-brand incubator my daughter was elegant.

"She's sleeping, Mommy," an NICU nurse told me. The nurses there call everyone "Mommy."

My daughter was attached to an IV drip for feeding. Lying on her side, she had a CPAP (continuous positive airway pressure) tube in one nostril to keep her lungs inflated. On her chest were penny-sized sticky pads holding down wires that were attached to a machine that measures heart rate, pulse, and oxygen level. Any time her oxygen level or heart rate became abnormal, bells would go off. There were forty babies in the NICU, and each was attached to monitors like these. With bells going off constantly, the place sounded like S. Klein's during a lingerie sale.

Dr. Holtzman came over to me as I looked at my baby from my wheelchair.

"She needs a name," he said.

"I'm working on it," I told him. "Names are a big deal to a playwright."

"Well, pick something. She's doing much better." He made a knocking-on-wood gesture. "She's a good kid even if she does look like you wouldn't pick her out in the poultry department."

"Thank you." I decided to take this as a compliment. He sees poultry. I see Audrey Hepburn.

The nipple Nazis attacked Tuesday at dawn.

"Are you pumping?" an ultra-thin woman was interrogating me from my doorway.

"Not yet," I answered. "I just had preeclampsia, a cesarean, and my daughter was born at twenty-seven weeks. I think I need to sleep."

"You must pump every three hours!" she announced. "Or you will dry up."

She wheeled in an industrial-strength breast pump that looked like it could bail out a battleship. Sternly, she showed me how to pump each breast separately or, if I liked, both together, a sort of duet for mammaries.

"Keep pumping every three hours and bring the milk upstairs to the fridge in the NICU," she said. She spoke so quickly I could hardly understand her, but it was clear that if I didn't do as she said, my baby and I would rot in hell.

"When your baby's ready, you can breast-feed her upstairs," she concluded.

"May I sleep tonight?" I asked.

"If you have to. You can miss one pumping." She left me with my own milk-master machine.

Duly intimidated, I tried to sit up and attach the two plastic bottles to my now Hindenburg-sized breasts. Hurricane Floyd was raging outside and my incision staples were piercing my stomach. As I was trying to pump, a social worker came into the room.

"Your mother is here," she said. "She doesn't know if you want to see her."

Bruce had told my mother about the birth. I still hadn't spoken to her. For most of my life my mother, who has the petite build of a Fosse dancer and sharp dark brown eyes, has told people that her age was "twenty-one plus." When her oldest granddaughter hit thirty, my mother became thirty too. Although I have given up even trying to estimate how old she is, what is clear is that my mother is a survivor. Even at thirty she takes Broadway dance classes every day. Lola is a trouper.

In my hospital room, my mother sat across from my bed wearing black leather pants, a multicolored sweater, and a bright knit cap. My father, in a gray suit, sat silently beside her.

"We saw the baby. She's very little," my mother said.

I continued eating orange Jell-O.

"We thought you didn't want to see us, but your father had an appointment here at gerontology."

"Are you OK, Dad?" I asked. I felt guilty.

"He's fine." Lola is my father's official spokesperson.

I looked at my mother. Her eyes were shining as if she were still a girl playing by the Vistula River in Poland.

"Mother, I want you to go back to see the baby and tell her you're her grandma." I took her hand. "I want you to pass your energy on to her. I want you to teach her how to survive!"

My mother dropped my hand. "She's my grandchild! Of course she'll survive!"

My sister Georgette later told me that when my mother first saw the size of my baby and heard the details of my delivery, she cried as inconsolably as she had when Sandra died.

"I have a name for my daughter," I announced to Dr. Holtzman five days after the delivery. I was examining a twinkling ruby light on my baby's big toe. The light was heating up her capillaries and tracking her blood pressure.

"Well, what's her name?" an Irish nurse with a long braid asked me.

"Lucy Jane," I answered, sort of testing the waters.

"I'm Catherine," the Irish nurse said. "I was the nurse who admitted your daughter and will be her primary care nurse during her stay here."

There are at least twenty nurses permanently on call at the NICU. They are constantly washing their hands, diapering tiny babies, and racing to incubators whose bells are ringing. None of them was more efficient than Catherine McCarron. Catherine works at the neonatal unit every weekend and on Mondays. During that time she cares for and feeds at least four premature babies and, perhaps even more difficult, deals with their mothers.

"Would you like to hold Lucy?" Catherine asked me that morning.

"Hold her?" I asked incredulously. Lucy Jane was attached to at least six wires and was the size of my outstretched hand. So far our contact had been through the incubator's porthole.

"It's called kangaroo care," she explained. "There was a study done in Colombia of premature babies who certainly didn't have the advanced medical advantages of a place like this. But a mother just holding her baby, skin to skin, made an enormous difference."

I washed my hands while Catherine opened the incubator. She handed me my daughter. Lucy Jane was almost weightless. Her tiny legs dangled like a doll's. Her diaper was the size of a cigarette pack. I opened my sweater and put her inside. Her face was smaller than an apple. She wore a tiny pink-and-blue striped cap that made her look like Santa's tiniest elf. I began to sing to her softly. "Picture yourself on a boat on a river where tangerine peaches meet marshmallow skies." I knew that those weren't exactly the right lyrics, but they were close enough. I told my daughter I named her Lucy because when she waved to me from the sonogram, I thought she was Lucy in the Sky with Diamonds, saying hello.

The bells in the NICU continued to ring. Mothers sat by their tiny infants, fighting for life in their Isolettes. I sat there among them, wanting my daughter to see a full moon and eat a fruit. Her nickel-sized feet tickled my breast. I couldn't cry in the NICU. We were there, I hoped, for the long haul.

Three weeks after I spoke at Fay Francis's funeral, Dr. Rebecca Brightman arrived in my hospital room to remove my staples and to tell me it was time for me to go home.

When I walked out of the Klingenstein Pavilion onto Fifth Avenue on the day before Yom Kippur, the city seemed to be in Technicolor. James Lapine and Heidi Ettinger, another friend from drama school, had come to take me home. Lucy would be staying in the NICU until at least December 14, my original due date. When I had checked into Mount Sinai, it was still summer, and now there were some autumn leaves on the trees. I watched as couples walked through the revolving doors holding their newborns in their required-by-law car seats. Those parents were satisfied customers. They got what they came for. I felt ashamed of envying them, after all I was alive, and so was Lucy. But I did envy them.

In the portable-sized Medela home pumping instruction book is a photo of a woman double-pumping her breasts and writing on a legal pad. She is my new hero. Not only is she a world-class "juggler," she managed to put the thing together. James Lapine and Heidi quickly gave up on it and called in the CBS producer.

An hour later Peter Schweitzer is sitting by my bed demonstrating what he calls "the cappuccino machine." Heidi and I tell him this is a new way for him to meet women. He could demonstrate door-to-door. How many bachelors are there in the La Leche society?

Heidi stays with me after both men leave. She asks me quietly if I'm all right now.

"Did you pump with all three of your children?" I whisper.

"I used to do it in the bathroom during previews for *Big River*," my old friend tells me, referring to the Broadway musical she designed.

"Do you want me to watch you?" she offers.

"Yes." I am both embarrassed and deeply grateful. I unbutton my blouse and put the plastic bottle to my breast. The milk starts dripping out. Heidi sits there like my sister.

A day after I arrived home there was a message on my answering machine from the NICU. Lucy Jane had needed a transfusion and the attending doctor wanted to notify me that they had used blood from the hospital bank. When I reached Catherine McCarron, she told me they had moved quickly because Lucy had become anemic and had turned pale.

After assuring me that everything was OK, she said, "I think I may also have overstepped myself slightly. Your mother happened to come in for a visit when the transfusion was happening, and I think it threw her." I imagined Lola grabbing her heart in agony and knocking over several Isolettes.

"She caused a little bit of a stir. So I hope you don't mind, but I asked her only to come with you or with scheduled permission. Is that all right?"

"Yes. It's fine. I'm sorry. Thank you, Catherine."

I hung up and called my mother.

"I hate that Irish nurse," Lola said. "Everyone else there loves me. But if you don't want me to go, I won't go."

"I want you to go, Mother," I said. "Just next time come with me."

That evening I walked up Madison Avenue to Yom Kippur services. I wondered if the congregation at Temple Emanu-El had heard yet that there was a restraining order against my mother at Mount Sinai.

A year earlier, my sister Sandra's name had been mentioned in memoriam by Rabbi Sobel during the Kol Nidre service. This year I was praying for my daughter. That's a lot of activity for a nonbeliever.

On the holiest night of the year, I took a taxi back to the Klingenstein Pavilion. It was ten o'clock and I learned that Lucy Jane had had another reversal. She had lost around fifty grams as a result of the transfusion, and now she had a respirator tube taped over her nose and mouth. My daughter, like some other critical babies in the NICU, was under a plastic container as if she were a hydroponic head of Bibb lettuce. She was also wearing a *What's My Line* eye mask. This was to shield her eyes from the bright lights that were installed in the Isolette to correct her high bilirubin levels, or jaundice.

I put my hand through the Isolette porthole and stroked her tiny fingers.

When I was in college, there was a popular aphorism: "Smith is to bed, Holyoke to wed." That sums up why my mother had been glad when I decided on Mount Holyoke. She thought I'd pick up a little art history plus a husband and security. But I've never understood how marriage offers a woman safety. Leaving the NICU that night, though, for the first time I felt how frightening going through all this alone was. For once I wished all the ridiculous myths were true: If a man in a suit could make this easier, I thought, I would happily return to Temple Emanu-El for an emergency Yom Kippur nuptial ceremony. But even a man in a suit is no guarantee against high bilirubin levels and anemia.

The NICU is a large open space divided in the front by a

long reception desk and ringed all around by a pink-and-blue wallpaper border of rabbits and teddy bears in hot-air balloons. The Isolettes are lined up against the walls with about four feet of room for a rocking chair between them. Usually the entire unit holds forty infants. The most critical babies are in the back area. The ratio of babies to nurses there is two to one. To the front on the left are the long-term tenants, preemies who will be staying a month or two, roughly until their natural due date. These children eat, sleep, and excrete until they reach four pounds, drink from a bottle, and can sleep five nights in an open-air crib. The ratio of infants to nurses here is four to one. To the right are the healthiest babies, the short-term residents. These babies tend to be twins with a touch of jaundice or full-term newborns with some small complication or low Apgar scores. For the most part, they're here on a special one-night plan or, at the most, the weeklong package deal.

Two weeks after Lucy Jane arrived in the NICU, Catherine announced to me that she was being promoted out of the critical nook.

"She's been able to breathe without the CPAP so they're putting her up front."

Lucy Jane Wasserstein's see-through mobile home was moved to the front left corner of the NICU. Living alongside Lucy was a baby whom I'll call Shayna Hutchinson. She was born a month before Lucy and now weighed approximately three pounds. Most preemies turn the corner when they weigh a kilo (2.2 pounds). Shayna had achieved that goal; Lucy was still working on it.

I recognized Shayna's mother, Miss Hutchinson, from our time in the back room, when our babies were still critical. A tall African-American woman, she guarded her daughter jealously. Miss Hutchinson asked the nurses to account for even the slightest change in her daughter's numbers. On Shayna's

Isolette was a sticker that read "Please call mother day or night with any news on her condition." At first Miss Hutchinson seldom said hello. In a nearby corner were Mrs. King, another African-American woman, and her son, and to her right were the Kaur twins, Tony and Tina, whose father owns an Indian restaurant on Columbus Avenue. Together with the Asian, Caribbean, and Irish nurses, our wing of the NICU redefined a multicultural neighborhood. Competitively, we'd all check out each other's babies' weight. Compassionately, we'd ask a nurse if everything was all right when a resonator or bilirubin light suddenly blinked on. In our zone, none of the babies, except for the Kaur twins, had a visible father.

There is a rhythm to visiting the NICU. I tried to go twice a day, mostly at feeding times, with my ready-to-go bottles of home-pumped milk. Once their lungs are strong enough, the babies move on from IVs to feeding through nasogastric tubes. Every three hours, mother's milk is pumped into a pipe-cleaner-sized tube that drips into the baby's nose. Most pree-mies have to build up the strength to suck from a bottle.

Arriving to see Lucy at 5:00 p.m. one night, I noticed that her tiny knit cap had been cut down the center.

"Why did they do that to Lucy's cap?" I asked one of the nurses. It was a weeknight and Catherine was off duty.

"They took another brain sonogram today," she informed me.

"Another!" I hadn't heard of the first one, and I panicked, just as my mother would have. "Is something wrong?" I asked.

"You'll have to ask the doctor. We can't reveal any information," she told me. I ran down the corridor in search of Dr. Green, a large southerner who was covering for Ian Holtzman. He was talking to a resident.

"I'm Lucy Jane Wasserstein's mother," I said, panting. "Can you tell me about her brain sonogram?"

"I'm in the middle of a sentence right now," he answered. Then he walked away.

With no information about Lucy, I couldn't bring myself to go back inside to those fluorescent lights, the ringing bells, and Mrs. Kaur endlessly knitting afghans for her twins. I couldn't bring myself to smile one more minute or pretend this was all just routine for me. I went home, got into bed, and cried.

Before I returned to the NICU in the morning, a friend called to warn me that there was a large item in a daily tabloid speculating about the identity of my child's father. During my entire hospital stay, no one asked me about this. Now suddenly I felt like Hester Prynne, and my daughter, who was in intensive care with a possible brain malfunction, was fodder for gossip columns.

The next morning at the hospital, I was able to talk to Dr. Holtzman.

"The brain ventricles are slightly enlarged but I wouldn't worry about it," he told me. "Most likely she'll just grow out of it. I'll do another sonogram on her myself and we'll follow it up next week."

I looked over at Shayna. She still had a CPAP in her nose to aid her breathing. Her brain was doing fine, though.

By this time Shayna and Lucy Jane were strong enough to drink from a bottle. There wasn't enough room in the corner of the NICU for Miss Hutchinson and me to feed our daughters at the same time, so I scheduled my visits around hers. During our time in the hospital, we managed to build a neighborly friendship.

"I think Lucy and Shayna leave here in the middle of the night and go out for pizza," I said one evening, trying to lighten both of our loads.

"I check on Lucy whenever I see Shayna," Miss Hutchinson said, laughing for the first time. "Those Latin women over there come snooping around here and I won't let them get near either of our babies."

I felt that with Miss Hutchinson guarding her, Lucy Jane was the safest she would ever be.

Dr. Green interrupted me as I was feeding Lucy one night.

"I want to talk to you!" he said. "She had another sonogram and the ventricles are still enlarged."

"Dr. Holtzman said there was no reason to worry," I said.

"I'm just warning you. We're sending her downstairs for another sonogram tomorrow."

At 8:00 a.m. I stood by my daughter's Isolette. When I was a child Lola would always kiss our *kepeleh* (the Yiddish word for "head") before any major test. I put my hand through the porthole and touched her head. "A kiss on the *kepeleh,* Lucy Jane," I whispered.

After the sonogram, I ran into a young professional-looking woman who had taken home one of her premature twins on a heart-lung monitor while the other remained in the NICU in critical condition.

"This is a very bittersweet place," she said, touching my shoulder. "It's wonderful having my daughter home, but the other one being here is very hard." In December, I learned that the twin in the NICU had not survived.

I was rocking Lucy in our corner of the NICU when Ian Holtzman came back with the test results, beaming.

"Not a problem," he told me. "Ventricles are completely normal!" He put up his hand for a high five. I slapped him back and kissed my daughter.

"She's doing great. I think she might be home before Thanksgiving," Dr. Holtzman went on. "You better get that crib ready."

During Lucy Jane's hospital stay, my brother visited her regularly. His son Dash arrived a week after she did, and he continued to flummox the hospital staff by saying that both babies were his children. I believe that his constant visits caused my daughter to become a very early overachiever.

A week before Thanksgiving Lucy Jane moved to the final, predischarge level of the NICU. We were now in the company of white professional couples who had conceived twins after taking fertility drugs. For the first time in the NICU I felt self-conscious about being a single mother.

"Would you like to feed Lucy Jane in the nesting room?" Catherine asked me.

I took my daughter, finally unattached by wires, to a private room where parents bond with their children in the days before they leave the NICU. As I rocked her, I whispered to her, "We are so lucky!"

Gerry Gutierrez came to the NICU on Lucy Jane's final night in residence. Catherine reminded me to bring a car seat tomorrow. I was going to be one of those parents in the revolving door.

I went over to Miss Hutchinson to say goodbye. "I brought something for Shayna," I said, and handed her a package. It was a doll and a children's book I had written.

Miss Hutchinson turned away. I reached toward her and she moved backward.

"I feel so badly," she said. "I didn't bring anything for you."

"That's all right," I said. "Shayna was Lucy Jane's first roommate." Miss Hutchinson began to cry. It was almost time for Shayna to go home, too.

Gerry and I took a taxi down Fifth Avenue, and I noticed that the city was lit up for Christmas.

"Miss Hutchinson wins best supporting actress in *The Birth of Lucy Jane*," Gerry said over dinner. The best supporting actor award, we decided, went to Dr. Rob Phillips. (I had learned a few weeks earlier that his group had been accepted to advise on missions to outer space. But contrary to my phenobarbital-enhanced assumptions, he wouldn't be taking blood pressure readings on Mars; he'd be consulting from Earth.) And the Jean Hersholt Humanitarian Award went to Lola Wasserstein.

James Lapine and Heidi Ettinger arrived at Mount Sinai in the morning to take me and Lucy Jane home. Catherine McCarron walked us to the door and cut off Lucy Jane's hospital bracelet, ten weeks after her birth. She gave me a kiss and said, "Once you get Lucy Jane home you'll forget all about this place."

"No, I will never forget this place," I told her.

A week after Lucy Jane came home I was walking down the street in my neighborhood and strangers smiled at me. "How's the baby?" they asked. A concierge at the Parker Meridien Hotel stopped me to say, "I think your having that baby is just great!" Suddenly I felt as if I were in a millennial version of *It's a Wonderful Life*. Hester Prynne had become the most popular girl in town.

While waiting at the Eastside Women's OB/GYN Associates for my final post-cesarean checkup, I picked up a magazine and found an article called "Cindy Crawford, Model Mom." Cindy was back at work. On the Web she had launched a monthly column recommending baby products. Cindy was having a ball.

Weeks earlier, Miss Hutchinson had told me, "Every night I pray for all the children here." I began to pray for them too. Although I remain a religious skeptic (St. James and Temple Emanu-El notwithstanding), throughout my days of awe at the Klingenstein Pavilion I had a kind of blind faith. I believed in the collaboration between the firm will of my one-pound-twelve-ounce daughter and the expertise of modern medicine. Of course, there was more than a bit of random luck involved too.

Just after a midnight feeding recently, Lucy Jane and I settled in to watch television. An *I Love Lucy* rerun was on. It was the one where Lucy has just had a baby and Ricky rushes to the maternity ward in his voodoo costume fresh from the Tropicana. When Ricky burst into song, my daughter started to cry. She had seen a lot of things in the NICU but she wasn't accustomed to bellowing Cuban men in feathers. I held her close— all ten pounds of her—and told her not to be frightened. Then I looked down at her double chin and her now pinchable baby cheeks. "I love Lucy, too," I told her. "And we're home."

A Note on the Type

The text of this book was set in Garamond No. 3. It is not a true copy of any of the designs of Claude Garamond (ca. 1480–1561), but an adaptation of his types, which set the European standard for two centuries. It probably owes as much to the designs of Jean Jannon, a Protestant printer working in Sedan in the early seventeenth century, who had worked with Garamond's romans earlier, in Paris, but who was denied their use because of Catholic censorship. Jannon's matrices came into the possession of the Imprimerie Nationale, where they were thought to be by Garamond himself, and were so described when the Imprimerie revived the type in 1900. This particular version is based on an adaptation by Morris Fuller Benton.

Composed by Creative Graphics,
Allentown, Pennsylvania

Printed and bound by Quebecor Printing,
Martinsburg, West Virginia

Designed by Iris Weinstein